Further praise for *How to Get the Perfect Promotion* by John Lees

'A lively and interesting guide aimed at informing and supporting individuals with career planning.'

**Deirdre Hughes, Director, Centre for Guidance Studies,
University of Derby**

'Job search within your organization! What a great and very sensible idea. John Lees' book is packed with practical hints to progress your career from within the organization.'

Robin Wood, MD, Career Management Consultants Limited

'John Lees gives practical advice to help you take control of advancing your career – now it's down to you!'

Joëlle Warren, MD of executive recruiters Warren Partners Ltd

Praise for *How to Get a Job You'll Love* by John Lees

'Offers a fresh look at career planning.'

The Guardian

'I am delighted with the revised edition. It is only if we enjoy and believe in our work that we have any chance, both of doing a good job and having a happy and satisfying life.'

Sir John Harvey-Jones MBE

'A rare combination of accessibility and thoughtfulness ... I whole-heartedly recommend it.'

Stephen Bampfylde, Chairman, Saxton Bampfylde Hever Plc

'A wonderful source of enthusiasm.'

Daniel Perot, International Careers Expert and Author

'I love its originality and thoroughness. Stimulates creative thinking and guides you thorough the job search process. We give copies to all our clients.'

Dr Harry Freedman, Director, Career Energy

How to Get the
Perfect Promotion

How to Get the Perfect Promotion

the complete guide to career development

John Lees

*The **McGraw·Hill** Companies*

London • Burr Ridge IL • New York • St Louis • San Francisco • Auckland
Bogotá • Caracas • Lisbon • Madrid • Mexico • Milan
Montreal • New Delhi • Panama • Paris • San Juan • São Paulo
Singapore • Sydney • Tokyo • Toronto

The McGraw·Hill Companies

How to Get the Perfect Promotion:
the complete guide to career development
First edition
John Lees

ISBN 0077104269

 **Professional**

Published by McGraw-Hill Professional
Shoppenhangers Road
Maidenhead
Berkshire
SL6 2QL
Telephone: 44 (0) 1628 502 500
Fax: 44 (0) 1628 770 224
Website: www.mcgraw-hill.co.uk

British Library Cataloguing in Publication Data
A catalogue record for this book is available from the British Library

Library of Congress Cataloguing in Publication Data
The Library of Congress data for this book has been applied for from the Library of
Congress

Text design by Robert Gray
Produced by Gray Publishing, Tunbridge Wells, Kent
Cover design by Two Associates Ltd
Printed and bound in UK by Clays Ltd, Bungay, Suffolk

About the Author

John Lees is a graduate of the Universities of Cambridge and London. He specializes in helping people to make difficult career decisions; difficult either because they don't know what to do next, or because there are barriers in the way to success.

Formerly Chief Executive of the Institute of Employment Consultants (now the Recruitment & Employment Confederation, REC), John has trained recruitment specialists for the last 15 years. He's become increasingly interested in the needs of people sitting on the other side of the desk: career changers.

John has undertaken career workshops in Europe, the USA and South Africa. He writes regularly on careers issues. He has a regular column in *The Times*, and his work has been featured widely in national newspapers and magazines. *How To Get A Job You'll Love* was WH Smith's Business Book of the Month in January 2003, and in the same year became the bestselling careers book by a British author.

He lives and works in Cheshire, with his wife, the children's writer Jan Dean, and their two teenage sons.

See www.johnleescareers.com for further materials and checklists, and for details of workshops and programmes run by John Lees Associates.

Thanks

While all the errors and omissions in this book are my own, my gratitude goes to all those whose feedback or ideas helped to shape this book, including: Stuart Robertson and Derek Wilkie of Stuart Robertson Associates, Revd Mary Leigh, Carole Pemberton and Ian Webb. Thanks to Janie Wilson and Mary Maybin of Passport for supporting some of the workshops where I road-tested these ideas. I would particularly like to thank Robin Wood, MD of Career Management Consultants Limited, for giving me the opportunity to test out many of these ideas with CMC's clients and consultants.

I am indebted to Stephanie Clark for her website research, and to Sue Blake for creating so many interesting conversations. Most of all I owe my editor Elizabeth Choules a huge thank you, not only for coaxing the book into existence with her usual diligence, but also for helping me to absorb the results of the survey featured in Chapter 2 of this book.

My thanks, too, to all those who responded to the career survey: Janet Basford, Marc J. Beaulieu, Penney Beazely, Peter Bell, Jo Bond, Sara Bosley, Andrew Bramley, June Burrough, Andrew Carr, Stuart Carter, Penny Chester, Linda Clark, Claire Coldwell, Andy Cole, Geoff Coombe, John Courtis, Samantha Csorba, Margaret Dale, Bill Douse, John Eardley, Ron Feasey, Nicola Foster, John Francis, Harry Freedman, Beverley Gartside, Helen Green, Keith Harden, Andrée Harpur, Rob Head, Bill Hollyhead, Rod Howgate, Deirdre Hughes, Stephen Hunter, Peter Jackson, Fred Mahoney, Stuart McIntosh, Jane Moorhouse, Breda O'Toole, Derek Osborn, Bernard Pearce, Daniel Porot, Lorraine Reynolds, Julia Robertson, Helen Rodway, Melissa Rosati, Alan Small, Philip Spencer, Rob Stickland, Anne Stojic, Alan Thurm, Garth Toombs, Mike Wallwork, Linda Walmsley, Bill Walmsley, Joëlle Warren, Ian Webb, Pegi Wheatley, Justine Wilkinson, Robin Wood and Doreen Wright.

This book is dedicated to my sons Matthew and Christopher, soon to step out into the career jungle.

Contents

About the Author   v

Preface   ix

Chapter 1

What Gets People Promoted?   1

Chapter 2

Insider Information: How Others Travelled
This Way Before You   18

Chapter 3

Your DIY Career Pilot Kit   40

Chapter 4

What Do You Mean By Success?   55

Chapter 5

Solving Employers' Problems: The Key
to Promotion Success   79

Chapter 6

Marketing Yourself Within the Organization   99

Chapter 7

Survive and Thrive   116

Chapter 8

Cutting a Great Deal   142

Chapter 9

Upward, Ever Upward?   158

Chapter 10

Stocking Your Lifeboat   180

Chapter 11

Making Your Mark in a New Job   200

Chapter 12

Breaks and Switches   214

Chapter 13

Steps Towards the Perfect Promotion   223

Useful Websites   232

Index   236

Preface

WHO IS THIS BOOK FOR?

This book is written for anyone who is trying to build a career. It's a tough job, and we are given very little preparation or training to help us along the way. However, there is a wide range of choices available to us, and we have far more control over our future than we may dare to think.

HOW THIS BOOK WILL HELP

If you've got a sense of what makes your job enjoyable, you will have a sense of how you can improve your job, achieve a promotion or negotiate a pay rise.

This book will help you if you aim to:

▌ achieve a promotion

▌ improve your pay and benefits package

▌ increase the skill level of your role

▌ increase the variety of your job

▌ delegate or ditch tasks you dislike

▌ change the way your boss sees you

▌ seek specific learning or skill development opportunities

▌ add more value to your organization

▌ take on new tasks and responsibilities

▌ perform well in a new job

▌ explore whether you stay where you are or change employer

HOW TO USE THIS BOOK

Most career books are about job search. This book's aim is to encourage you to build your job up from the inside, to seek better and more effective ways of adding value to your organization, and to help you to negotiate the right mix in terms of job content, pay and, if that's where you want to go, to achieve promotion.

The chapters ahead approach one major issue: your career. You may find the one tool that unlocks your potential, or you may gain multiple insights from using several ideas or exercises. One word of advice: if the exercise doesn't work for you, don't feel you have 'failed'. All it means is this: *the exercise doesn't work for you*. Put it aside and move on.

The book begins by asking the general question **What Gets People Promoted**?, and exploring the choices that are available to you in Chapter 1.

A great deal of the focus of this book is on the results of a survey of senior managers and others with considerable experience of the factors that get people promoted. The key findings are summarized in Chapter 2, **Insider Information: How Others Travelled This Way Before You**.

Chapter 3 turns the spotlight on you, providing you with **Your DIY Career Pilot Kit**. Chapter 4 gives you the opportunity to define success in your own terms, and work out what motivates you.

For this thinking to be most practical, it also needs to focus on the needs of your employer. Chapter 5, **Solving Employers'**

Problems, checks out how familiar you are with the main concerns and goals of your organization.

Moving your way systematically towards a promotion requires a wide range of tools. Chapter 6 is a **Self-marketing Guide**, revealing a range of skills for communicating your strengths to the people that matter. Chapter 7, **Survive and Thrive**, offers help if you're in an organization that's downsizing or restructuring, encouraging you to move from survival mode to job growth, and at the same time looking at your overall life/work balance.

Next, some very practical tips for taking action. **Cutting a Great Deal** (Chapter 8) offers an extensive strategy for negotiating a pay rise. Chapter 9, **Upward, Ever Upward?** focuses on a different kind of negotiation – securing a promotion.

How do you know when it's time to move on? Chapter 10, **Stocking Your Lifeboat**, explores when and how to think about seeking opportunities outside the organization.

Chapter 11 focuses on **Making Your Mark in a New Job**, and will be useful to you if you're at that stage now, or when you next start a new role.

Chapter 12, **Breaks and Switches**, explores the wider range of career options available to you including retraining and career breaks, drawing upon the results of a recent opinion poll.

The book closes with two highly practical stages. Chapter 13 provides you with **Steps Towards the Perfect Promotion**, while Chapter 14 provides you with a list of useful websites providing hundreds of tips about career development, negotiating a pay rise and finding your ideal career.

What Gets People Promoted?

This chapter helps you to:

▌ Understand how and why people move up the career ladder

▌ Look at better methods of shaping your career

▌ Find strategies for taking control of your future

▌ Audit how satisfied you are with your present job

▌ Begin your path to promotion

Manage your future or somebody else will.

Peter Drucker

WHY AND HOW PEOPLE GET PROMOTED

Unless you have a relative who owns the company, no-one starts out at the top. We have to get there using some kind of strategy. Companies create the idea that all you have to do is work hard and keep your nose to the grindstone, and all will be well. Yet we all know that the most hard-working, or the most competent, are not always the ones who receive promotion.

At one time skills made the difference. The ability to operate a particular machine or manage a particular process gained you a pay premium. Automation has largely solved the problem of tasks that take a long time to learn. For example, 20 years ago it required a fairly specialized knowledge of software to produce spreadsheets. Now, personal computers contain detailed 'help' functions that can assist even the novice user to get results quickly. IT skills are possessed by a huge number of people, and so are highly developed people skills such as influencing, persuading and coaching. Skills alone are no longer enough.

When new employees join an organization, they often assume that the way up the career ladder is to sit tight and do a great job, thereby working their way up step by step. Some will discover that those who find an unconventional route leapfrog their way to the boardroom: a matter of finding supporters, speaking the right language and reading the runes, combined with a strong focus on the next right step. And, undoubtedly, a strategy for coping with failure and moving on quickly. These people know the difference between things they can change and the factors that are outside their control.

Ask your friends and colleagues how and why people get promoted. Listen carefully to their responses. If you get the opportunity, ask successful people how they got promoted, and ask for their advice on what others should do.

I conducted a survey of senior and middle managers, consultants, training specialists and business owners. I asked them four key questions:

1. What one key action or event can you identify as a formative step in building your career?

2. What is the best approach/strategy/activity to gain a promotion?

3. What behaviours and attitudes at work get staff promoted?

4. What one piece of advice you would give to someone who wants to achieve a promotion at work in the next 12 months?

The answers are dealt with in a lot more detail in Chapter 2, and suggest the following key characteristics, in rank order:

1. Being self-aware

2. Being more aware of the needs of the organization

3. Displaying the right behaviours and attitudes

4. Influencing key people in the organization

5. Pushing the boundaries of your job

6. Having the right skills and know-how

7. Working hard

8. Being in the right place at the right time.

What's significant here is that hard work and skills are seen as important, but nowhere near as important as factors 1 to 5. However, this realization normally leads people to two major fallacies: that getting promoted is about being lucky or about toadying up to the boss.

Being in the right place at the right time is very occasionally about pure luck or blind chance. It's far more commonly about being in tune with what an organization is trying to achieve. On one level this is why those achieving fast-track promotions are often the people who look the part, speak the right language and go to the right meetings. The organization has developed a picture of the future executive and these individuals are a strong match. This has very little to do with chance. Instinctively, or consciously, these are staff who have made their 'offer' match the current and future needs of the organization. The company feels good about having these people around. They get promoted.

What kind of promotion?

You may be looking for the next, obvious step up the ladder, or ready to make a much bigger leap. You may want to move into a job slightly bigger than the one you've got, or something much bigger. Table 1.1 shows some different promotion possibilities. How many of them have you *really* considered?

Table 1.1 Promotion possibilities

Promotion possibility	Key thinking
Moving from a temporary or contract post to a permanent position	You have a great chance of doing this just by sticking around, getting to know the right people, and by looking and sounding just like someone who already works there.
Moving from an unskilled or a semi-skilled entry level position to a skilled position	Show interest, energy and a hunger to learn, and at the same time don't neglect your present job. Your willingness to improve processes and efficiency (without treading on the toes of your supervisor) will quickly communicate potential. Ask about the minimum entry standards for the next role, and how much flexibility there is around qualifications or experience.
Moving into the next grade up from your present level	What know-how do you need to demonstrate to be considered suitable for this role? If there are company rules and expectations about time served, age or experience, actively seek out examples where these rules have been bent.
Moving into a significantly more senior role	Again, look for examples where others have done this before you. What skills or specialist knowledge did they demonstrate? How did they behave? How were they seen by the organization?
Moving into a supervisory or management position	Seek opportunities to train, develop and monitor other members of staff. How have others made this leap before you? Are you availing yourself of the full range of training available to you? What can you learn outside the job?

Moving into a higher status role in another department or organization	How far have you put together a record of your relevant achievements? How are you going to convince managers who don't know you well that you have the confidence and potential to cope with a change of context *and* greater responsibility?
Leapfrogging one level or more into a senior job	Don't be put off by company rules and the way things are normally done. Companies break promotion rules all the time to get the right results. Seek out high-fliers who have done this before you; look at their strategies and behaviours. Most importantly, don't neglect to ask for the opportunity, no matter how ambitious.
Influencing your employer to create a new job around you	This is far more likely than you think. Begin by taking on projects where you can demonstrate initiative and achieve results quickly. Seek out clear opportunities to match your employer's Key Result Areas (see Chapter 5).
Going for the top	This is not one for those who lack conviction and do not convey great credibility. You will have to hunt more doggedly for examples of people who have done this, and closely track the way they moved up the organization. What is usually most informative is to look at the first two or three career steps that these business leaders followed, and then look in detail at the characteristics, strategies (and costs) of getting to the boardroom.

Leapfrogging

It's very rare that a career plan works out exactly as you have planned it, but that shouldn't prevent you trying. Talk to those who have made rapid career progression, and you will often find that they have found some way of subverting or bypassing traditional career routes. It's often just a question of asking 'What other ways are there?' Seek out examples of where colleagues have leapfrogged over particular grades or roles. You may find that this has happened because of a combination of a particular organizational need and their own, well-communicated strengths.

Becoming promotable

Jamie worked as department head in a school which was interested in leading the field as far as pastoral and social education was concerned. He was asked to put together a conference on citizenship and to invite interested parties. He realized that he had a good chance of attracting funding if he managed to convince major organizations to attend – the local authority, large local employers, national research organizations. He was able to circulate a cheap but effective conference folder which included their corporate logos. He made sure that his head teacher and several key governors had key roles either speaking at or hosting key sessions. By finding a strong, well-funded topic of interest, convincing the right people to give their names to the project, and reflecting a great deal of the limelight to senior staff and governors, Jamie transformed the image that key decision makers had of him. He was quickly able to move to head of faculty, and shortly afterwards was being considered for another rapid move to deputy head.

In a sense, getting promoted is very straightforward. In the words of one career change specialist: *'Promotable people are good at what they do and get results'*.

But being good at what you do isn't enough. You need to create visible results that are noticed by the organization. And not just by the organization, but by key decision makers in the organization: people who can create jobs, authorize promotions and influence your future.

Consider doing the OBVIOUS

Being promotable is therefore about achieving results that are OBVIOUS:

Observable: others will be talking about what you have achieved

Benchmarked: measurable in their effects

Visible to key decision-makers

Individual: your personal contribution will be clearly identifiable.

On Target: focused on what matters to the organization

Understood: people see the obstacles you had to overcome

Special: something that clearly differentiates you from others, whether external or internal to the organization.

To expand on the obvious, so to speak, we need to look at a breakdown of the different success factors involved, as Table 1.2 demonstrates.

Table 1.2 Factors that make you promotable

1 Be visible	Don't hide your light under a bushel. Does anyone notice you're doing a great job? If not, who is responsible?
2 Demonstrate initiative	Move out of passive mode. Look at opportunities to actively offer ideas and suggestions.
3 Go the extra mile	Become known as the kind of person who puts in just slightly more effort or energy than expected.
4 Underpromise and overdeliver	It's a principle that works well inside organizations as well as with customers.
5 Expand your job function	This isn't something you can do overnight, but find ways of gradually adding new tasks and responsibilities.
6 Achieve measurable results	Everyone claims to be doing a good job, but how can you demonstrate that in measurable terms? Think of appropriate measures you can use: financial, time, quality, company reputation, etc.
7 Achieve Key Results	Focus on the things that really matter to your employer, and what will make a difference. Identify the expected and actual Key Result Areas in the job.
8 Go for a mix of quick wins and long-term wins	Quick wins are sometimes easy and usually very effective in getting you permission to begin long-term projects.
9 Communicate your wins	Find a modest but honest way of communicating your successes. Who needs to know? What kind of message do they need to hear? Can you express your wins in meaningful terms?
10 Be self-motivating and a self-starter	Don't always rely on others to give you a 'go' light, or wait for someone to tell

	you exactly what to do, and how to do it. Begin to organize your own workload as far as you can. Learn how to motivate yourself to undertake tasks on the edge of your comfort zone.
11 Have a positive attitude, even under pressure	Don't give in to corporate cynicism. You don't have to become a smiling zombie, but don't be drawn into every cynical conversation.
12 Develop a 'try it and see' philosophy	Where others predict failure, encourage open experimentation.
13 Take responsibility, and do what you say	Your total work contribution may be judged by your ability to do what you promise. Take responsibility when you don't fulfil your commitments; look at how things could have worked better rather than blame others.
14 Behave like an adult	Learn how to say what you need and what you want to get out of work. Be direct and open, not covert and manipulative.
15 Be a strategic thinker	Don't get so obsessed by the perspective of your job that you lose track of the big picture.
16 Take time to learn and acquire knowledge	You will only achieve some critical steps by paying proper attention to your personal learning so you pick up skills and know-how.
17 Become known as an information broker	In a world overflowing with data, information brokers know where to lay their hands on critical knowledge.
18 Help others along the way	This isn't just about you. If you are a person who enables people and organizations to do their best, you help others to get the best out of their jobs, too.

Continued

19 Develop a network	You can only achieve the above steps with the help of others.
20 Seek voluntary opportunities	Particularly with causes that are supported by your employer. However, seek hands-on roles rather than leadership positions – demonstrate that you're interested in contributing, not just assisting your career goals.
21 Don't give up at the first barrier	All of the above steps can be problematic. Don't use that reality as an excuse for not starting to regenerate your job.

See also Chapter 9 for the reverse of these factors: career-limiting actions.

TAKING CONTROL OF YOUR FUTURE

Thinking about promotion prospects isn't just thinking about your next step up. It's about moving into a job which is more interesting, where you will learn and grow because you have greater responsibilities. It's about being stretched. To achieve that, you have to know what kind of work is right for you in the future.

How passive is your career plan?

How much does your future depend on the intervention of others – your boss, your colleagues, human resources? If your strategy is to sit tight, keep your head down and work hard, that might just work. However, you're not doing much to improve the odds. Being passive about our career futures is a tried and tested model, and you may be put under some pressure to conform to it: *don't rock the boat, don't draw attention to yourself, just keep your head down ...*

The passive model is the one we inherited from a time when employers did your career thinking for you: organized your training, planned your promotion steps, looked after your interest. Sixty years ago the idea that you had any real influence over your career, working hours, conditions or duties was completely alien to Western culture. You did the job, and you worked through until you got a pension. Employers essentially offered workers a 'deal': give us your hard work and your loyalty, and we'll give you job security and a future. This 'psychological contract' broke down somewhere in the 1990s after countless rounds of downsizing, 'rightsizing' and restructuring.

> Bill worked for a water board as a surveyor. He enjoyed some aspects of the job, but felt he was overqualified for the role. Occasionally more senior jobs became vacant, but after being turned down for one he was reluctant to press any further. If they want me for the job they'll invite me to apply, he thought. Finally a career step came in sight: his boss's retirement, 5 years away. All Bill had to do was work hard and wait for the job to fall into his lap. 12 months before his boss's retirement day the water authority was privatized. Bill was made redundant after his post was contracted out.

The world of work has changed and we have an interestingly uncomfortable new balance: we expect more from our careers in terms of personal rewards, and at the same time have taken up far more responsibility for our own futures. We change jobs more regularly than we did 25 years ago, but we also change occupations; in the USA, for example, it's now fairly common for workers to change career, not just job, three times or more in a working lifetime. Chapter 12 looks at some up-to-date UK research on this topic.

Today, the idea that you can do something about your career means something. To get the right promotion, you need to know what you want to add to your present role, and what you want to reduce. Therefore you need to know important things about the way you work, and also learn from others who have gone before you.

Look at top performers

Following a path that leads to promotion and a stimulating, responsible job is about understanding the characteristics and behaviours of people who:

- communicate how they closely match the needs of the organization (see Chapters 5 and 6)

- learn how to adapt their jobs, and keep on improving them (see Chapter 8)

- learn how to position themselves for promotion (see Chapter 8)

- find an ever-increasing range of ways of showing how they add value to the organization (see Chapter 5)

- understand how they are perceived by others (see Chapter 6)

- establish key relationships with influencers (see Chapter 6) and make sure they are visible within their organization

- develop their own careers and know when it's time to jump ship (see Chapter 10).

Why do people fail to get promoted?

First of all, promotion isn't a right. There are very few organizations that promote simply on the basis of time served or qualifications achieved. Secondly, every organization is a pyramid, in the sense that there are far more opportunities at the bottom than at the top. However, companies sometimes fail to retain key staff, and people leave the organization for a variety of reasons.

But be careful of using time as your main strategy: *'I'll stick at the job and work hard, and in time it'll get me promoted'*. It probably won't. The reason is that the strategy and the timescale are only evident to you. Decision makers are usually very focused on what you have to offer now, not your long-term history. Loyalty, working hard and having a great attendance record are important factors, but far less so than communicating your strengths in an immediate, accessible way.

After *waiting things out*, the nation's second favourite career strategy is probably this: *jumping at the first opportunity that comes along*.

This has its merits, especially if it's the opportunity of a life-time. But again it's a very passive strategy, this time letting chance events guide your future. Many senior executives tell me that their CV was effectively composed by opportunity rather than by active choice.

A more dynamic approach is to define what you are looking for, by developing a personal wish list. This will include your primary motivators, your skills, an understanding of the way that your personality fits the workplace, and where you want to get to.

Your final strategy if you want to ensure that you *don't* get promoted is to make sure that you carry out as many Career-Limiting Actions as possible. See Chapter 9 for more details.

EXERCISE 1.1 – AUDITING YOUR PRESENT ROLE

For the moment we are going to focus on the steps that you should take to increase your chances of moving up.

We start by analysing the overall fit of your job. Which areas of your job don't cut it for you? What do you really enjoy about your present role? Complete the audit in Table 1.3.

Table 1.3 Auditing your present role

Place an appropriate score on each line

Negative characteristics	
This description is true ... Most of the time 3 points Some of the time 2 points Hardly ever 1 point Not at all 0 points	
1 I am underemployed	
2 I am not using my skills	
3 I am not learning new skills	
4 The job doesn't challenge me	
5 I feel uncomfortable with the people I work alongside	
6 I dislike the way I am managed	
7 I dislike the way things are done at work	
8 I feel trapped in the job	
9 I feel I have very different values to my employer/others at work	
10 I feel undervalued at work	
11 I feel like calling in sick or avoiding work	
12 I complain about my job	
Total negative score	

Positive characteristics		
This description is true ...	Most of the time Some of the time Hardly ever Not at all	3 points 2 points 1 point 0 points
13 I have fun at work		
14 Work is interesting and absorbing		
15 I feel I would do the same job for half the money		
16 The job has variety		
17 I enjoy working with the people around me		
18 I have some influence over outcomes or the way things are done		
19 I feel I make a difference		
20 I feel my role is a very good match to my skills		
21 My boss delegates to my strengths		
22 I have a sense of progress in the job		
23 I have a chance to learn new ideas, techniques or skills		
24 I talk positively to my friends about my job		
Total positive score		

Examine your results from Table 1.3. Which score is greater: positive or negative? If you are scoring more than 25 or so on your negatives, clearly you need to do some work on your role, and this may be an important piece of preliminary work before you actively seek promotion.

A role that is a good match to your interests and personality is likely to give you a positive score that is 10–15 points higher than your negatives. If your overall score is positive, you have some great starting points for getting the perfect promotion, because you will be building on good relationships, and a role that is a good match to you. It should also be clear to you that you already have a number of positive areas to communicate.

Which parts of your job interest you, or even inspire you? What would you like to do more of? Are you using skills that you *enjoy* using? How will a promotion be more than just a move up the ladder, but a way of shaping a role that allows you to work even better?

Does work satisfaction matter when you're seeking promotion? Just work out for a moment how many hours you are likely to spend in work during the course of a working lifetime. typically about 100,000. That's an awfully long time to be watching the clock. Over 75 per cent of our weekly energy may be focused on work: preparing for work, getting to work, talking about work and worrying about work ...

The good news is that you can do a huge amount for yourself by taking active control, and it doesn't mean changing jobs.

Olivia has been temping in her organization for 4 months. She feels underemployed. She can see people with poorer qualifications than she has enjoying well-paid roles. On the verge of asking for an assignment somewhere else, Olivia was offered a choice: do nothing and stay as a temp, or move to another organization, or actively seek help. She chose the last choice, seeking a meeting with her line manager. She was surprised to hear that she was a valued member of the team, and that she had introduced several new ideas that had improved systems in the organ-ization. Furthermore, although this employer doesn't normally offer career development support for temps, in this case it was prepared to reinvent the rules. She now has several internal meetings lined up with managers, firstly to find out more about the organization, and secondly to investigate the possibility of permanent jobs.

'MUST DO' LIST

10 foundation steps for your promotion strategy

☑ Look at the positives and negatives in your present role. What can you change quickly? What can you change in the long term?

☑ What should your new role feel like in terms of work satisfaction?

☑ Write down your answer to the question: *'What benefits do I bring to my job?'* Ask yourself how far your employer shares the same perspective.

☑ Start putting together a portfolio which demonstrates where you added valued or made a difference.

☑ Talk to others in the organization about the jobs they do. Find out the people and the activities that really shape outcomes.

☑ Seek out pathfinders: people who have taken your chosen path before you. Learn from their mistakes, and from their enthusiasm.

☑ Write a detailed picture of your ideal job (boss, team, problems, opportunities, work environment, skills).

Insider Information: How Others Travelled This Way Before You

This chapter helps you to:

▌ Understand how others achieved career success

▌ Spot the pitfalls on the way

▌ Gain insights into how people achieve above-average career progression

▌ Identify attitudes and behaviours that get you promoted

▌ See that successful careers don't happen by accident

Work as if you'd been already promoted.

Daniel Porot

What makes people successful in their work and achieve promotion? In this chapter we are going to look in depth at the results of a career survey before moving, in later parts of the book, to look in more depth at how and why people are successful in careers, and what you can do about moving your own career forward.

There are many different ways of defining a successful career. I conducted a survey among a wide range of business professionals, all of them people who had achieved significant promotion in their careers. Many of them are now in senior positions or running their own businesses. The survey (there were 60 respondents in total) was not designed to produce hard statistics, but to mine the insights and wisdom of a combined work experience of well over 1200 years. Some of those surveyed have changed careers recently, others have been established in their roles for many years. Most are over 40. What they all have in common is significant business and management experience, plus an insight into the way their career came together.

Respondents to the survey were asked four simple questions:

1. What one key action or event can you identify as a formative step in building your career?

2. What is the best approach/strategy/activity to gain a promotion?

3. What behaviours and attitudes at work get staff promoted?

4. What single piece of advice you would give to someone who wants to achieve a promotion at work in the next 12 months?

Q1. WHAT ONE KEY ACTION OR EVENT CAN YOU IDENTIFY AS A FORMATIVE STEP IN BUILDING YOUR CAREER?

The majority of the respondents were able to identify a specific incident such as returning to a particular occupation, choosing to undertake a specific kind of training, returning to full-time education or being headhunted. Some respondents offered more general comments such as moving around and having a variety of jobs.

Comments in response to this question fell into a number of broad categories, as listed in Table 2.1, from A, the most common response (approximately 25 per cent) to E (under 10 per cent of responses).

Table 2.1 Key actions or events identified as formative career-building steps

Category	Key action/event
A	Self-awareness, a realization about yourself/role/company/manager/your abilities
B	Good supportive network including a sponsor/mentor
C	Returning to full-time study or education
D	Understanding and achieving corporate goals
E	Applying for promotion

Self-awareness/realization

Interestingly, in response to a question about key actions or events, most answers related not to action but to self-perception: coming to a new realization about your abilities and strengths, or a better picture of how you fit into the organization.

Careers consultant Claire Coldwell sums this up as (1) knowing yourself, and (2) knowing what the industry needs: 'If you're aware of your strengths and weaknesses and you understand how others see you, and you can maximize the former and develop the latter to address the issues which you see the industry is facing, then you'll be ahead of the game. Both of these require some effort, but if you enjoy your job, that's not too difficult.'

About a quarter of respondents placed some kind of self-awareness as their critical step. Responses covered a number of ways in which respondents became more self-aware. For many, this is a realization of what you *don't* like doing, and the skills you enjoy using.

Pegi Wheatley, owner of McCall Staff Services in San Francisco, found that she could turn a natural ability into a career. She describes this as 'Happening into a field that didn't seem like work', and goes on to explain: 'I am a curious person, too impatient and spontaneous to be politic or play office politics. Plus I'm a natural "chatterer" – I'm always striking up conversations with strangers everywhere, curious to understand their situation (whether employment, love life, or home decor) and then I love to dole out advice. In a corporation, "chatterers" aren't encouraged; structure is, time efficiency is. Being organized with paper and deadlines are valued. In job placement chatting to people is how you learn about where to place them or, in the case of a client, what it's like where they work, who will fit in.'

Career coach Derek Osborn, formerly a senior operational manager with the Post Office, draws upon a familiar saying when he recalls 'I needed to take control of my career and not wait for my boat to come in – rather swim out to it.' Other critical steps included an individual's exposure to a really exciting role, and a number of transitional roles managing projects or covering for illness or maternity leave.

Equally interesting is the realization for some that they could do the job better than their superior. One senior RAF officer discovered he was continually bailing out his manager, and so eventually took the plunge and successfully went for promotion himself.

One manager simply answered 'Awareness of company unwritten codes and cultures and working to them'. The emphasis is on the *unwritten* aspect – learning to switch on your radar to work out what really is going on in an organization.

Outplacement consultant Ron Feasey's key event was 'Being lucky enough for someone in the senior echelons to become a supporter/fan/promoter despite my limitations. Probably because we were both enthusiasts for the task. The moral is probably "Value/use/respect/relate to your seniors – they may not be as daft as you think!"'

Alan Small, while working as a product manager in a large multinational, transformed the way that his company saw him when he challenged the results of his annual appraisal which damned him with faint praise: 'I insisted on getting clarification on the criteria used in judging me and was given a month to demonstrate that the view of me in the appraisal was not valid. (This happens frequently with quiet people, where 'quiet' is taken to be the same as 'soft'. I had to persuade my masters that 'firm' was every bit as effective as 'loud' and often much more acceptable.)'

Finding support

Further down the list but still of significance is the topic 'Having a supportive network'. For some this was about having a sponsor or mentor, a senior and influential figure who could champion your case. Having friends, family or colleagues who were prepared to listen was also important, particularly if they are the kind of people who believed in you, see potential in you and encourage you to try new things. Some answers praised companies that had good training programmes and invested heavily in their personnel.

Requalifying

It was surprising how many people (approximately 15 per cent) went back into some form of education as a step to building their career. These included doing an MBA, CIPD or Diploma in Training Management. In some instances the desired role required them to take a specific course; in others education was seen as a means of widening horizons. Chapter 12 looks at retraining and career breaks in more detail.

Others found ways of taking on additional responsibilities and learning new things. Canadian outplacement consultant Garth Toombs saw learning as a key to building his career: 'leaving a job was often stimulated by feeling I had gone as far as I could or wanted to in the role.'

In some cases, new or extra responsibility was not an active choice. Rob Head, former Corporate Development Manager of Octel Corp., tells how a reallocation of roles disturbed his equilibrium and changed his career: 'My background to my early 30s was in R&D and I was good at that role with plenty of publications and some key patents. The thing that changed my career aspirations was being put into a small team with responsibility for investigating the market needs. This involved my making cold calls, and talking end user needs and not technology. It took me out of my comfort zone, gave me a fresh view of why technology was important, and I loved it.'

John Eardley spent over 30 years with ICI: 'In my case it was the decision, aged 27, to give up teaching and join ICI. I realized that I wasn't ever going to be the excellent, dedicated teacher that I so admired, and it would take a long time to become a headmaster. I decided to give industry 5 years, and then review my situation while I still had options. I stayed in ICI 30 years, in two different businesses and had eleven different jobs.'

Understanding and achieving company goals

This was seen a key to a number of respondents. Peter Bell, one time General Manager with United Co-operative, had regular meetings with the owners of the company he was headhunted to. This created a 'mutually favourable impression that resulted in a strong working understanding of goals and what it means to achieve them.'

Publishing executive Melissa Rosati reports: 'The first 10 years of my career occurred during merger mania. I've been on the buyer and the seller side of things. Either way, I took the approach of "never be bitter". I just looked at how I could turn the change and confusion to my advantage.'

Executive recruiter and careers author John Courtis' advice is: 'Doing things right and on time or telling peers and boss IN ADVANCE if it cannot be done thus. Making constructive suggestions promptly rather than whingeing later is good too. Be a "can do" person when it's possible and be sure to tell people crisply if they're asking the impossible or the unnecessary. You'll build respect from the people who matter.'

Applying for promotion

This is also tied up with raising your profile. Two respondents applied for promotion but were unsuccessful. However, in making the application, they both raised their profile so that they were either headhunted or considered for the next post.

One respondent highlighted that it was only when goals and delivery requirements were confirmed in writing with her CEO that she achieved her promotion.

For Robin Wood, MD of Career Management Consultants, tenacity was the key: 'Setting clear criteria for the "right" next position and sticking doggedly to them throughout 12 months of frustrating but determined job search.'

Other key factors included:

▮ Moving and gaining experiences in a variety of businesses, but also being prepared to relocate and live in different countries

▮ Being prepared to take a risk, e.g. self-funding a plane ticket to USA for a job interview, or leaving a secure job to start a new business

▮ Work/life balance. For some respondents ill-health required drastic action.

Q2. WHAT IS THE BEST APPROACH/STRATEGY/ACTIVITY TO GAIN A PROMOTION?

The majority of respondents talked about using a combination of different strategies. For example, HR consultant Anne Stojic: 'I believe the key is to build relationships and make an impression with the right people ... However I would also say it is important to anticipate what skills/experiences are required for the next promotion and work towards these in advance. In the past I have asked to attend training courses and also asked for extra responsibilities at work, this way before long you are doing a higher level job anyway.'

Responses fell into a number of general categories, as outlined in Table 2.2.

Table 2.2   The best approach/strategy/action to gain a promotion

A	Doing a good job
B	Getting noticed
C	Working upwards
D	Building networks
E	Understanding organizational politics
F	Finding a sponsor

Doing a good job

Over half of respondents suggested, perhaps unsurprisingly, that 'doing a good job' was the best strategy. This included the need to move outside the parameters of your job description, going the extra mile, and what one respondent called 'being solutions rather than problems'.

Many felt it was also very important to have a clear understanding of your job, goals and responsibilities: 'Know your company, its products/services, your colleagues and do your job particularly well', stated Rod Howgate, Founding Partner of recruitment consultancy Howgate Sable. 'Demonstrate a little more commitment than that portrayed by those peers around you', suggested Communications Director Mike Wallwork.

A couple of respondents specifically mentioned that you should ensure that your superiors are kept informed and never surprised by events. Chapter 9 tells you a lot more about managing your relationship with your boss.

Getting noticed

Working hard on its own was considered not enough to gain a promotion. You need to be noticed by the right people, the decision makers: 'Apart from doing a good job and delivering results, it is making sure that someone (preferably as many as possible) in a position of influence knows it' (outplacement consultant Bill Holyhead).

Over 25 per cent suggested that 'getting noticed' was a powerful component. Many suggested that the key is understanding the job fully and then working hard to ensure you are noticed. One respondent did throw in the caution 'ensure that one's seniors are aware of one's good work without antagonizing one's peers' (Ron Feasey). There seems a great deal of evidence to suggest that self-marketing should not be an individualistic activity: managers like teams rather than solo players.

It is important to be noticed for the right reasons, and one 'incident' may have drastic results: 'Critical incidents can both create and block opportunities for promotion. One company talked about why they released a particular manager. They had a number of recent reasons for the action, but a lot of their argument for making the decision centred around an incident which had happened 10 years earlier, where this employee had been inebriated at a company party and had been rude to the wife of the president' (Garth Toombs).

Mike Wallwork cited that it was important to 'have opinions and your own mind. Most people seem to respond more favourably to those that have an opinion than those that follow other "corporate" views.'

Having good personal qualities was seen as key by many people: 'be professional in all that you do and become the kind of person people can trust and rely on. Don't undermine others, give credit where it's due' (careers coach Rob Stickland). Other suggestions included 'Make friends at all levels and enemies at none – treat others as you would want to be treated' (executive recruiter Joëlle Warren).

Working upwards

'Working upwards' is, essentially, identifying the skills and experience that are required for the next promotion and actively building them into your CV. Looking and behaving like you have been promoted helps: 'I took to noting those qualities in those above me which make them particularly good either in their job or as leaders. I then sought to emulate them, wherever possible, and without aping them, did what they were doing, only better' (RAF selector Keith Harden). Life Coach Beverley Gartside suggests that 'it helps if you are already seen to be operating at the level to which you aspire.'

Keeping your eyes and ears open to opportunities was seen as very important: 'try to avoid saying no to good opportunities, recognizing that you can usually negotiate on any unsatisfactory elements of roles and jobs' (John Eardley).

Linda Walmsley, executive recruiter and former newspaper advertising executive, found it helpful 'offering to help with anything else that was going on in the department. Two benefits – I really enjoyed learning about someone else's role and pressures and they had more time for me in my current job because I had given them some help.'

One response suggested that if you are going to make yourself indispensable, do so with general transferable skills rather than skills restricted to a particular job, as you may get stuck there.

Networking

Networking and making good impressions seemed to go hand in hand in some respondents' minds, for example, 'build relationships and make an impression with the right people'. This was seen as critical when applying for top jobs. At very senior levels promotions are not always advertised and it is therefore essential to make sure that your name is known by those who might be asked to suggest suitable candidates.

Understanding organizational politics

The majority of respondents who made comments that fell into this category were of the opinion that you needed to be aware of and work the system, for example, 'think about the people who have power and influence in the organization, find out what makes them tick.'

Another key consideration was knowing how to feed information to your boss. The issue of how to manage your boss came up a number of times: 'learn to manage your boss, make your boss look good to their boss' (Joëlle Warren). At times this is about understanding and building on your boss's motivations of fear and greed: 'Make your boss think they are vulnerable because you are about to go somewhere else. Alternatively, deliver something so valuable to them that they put themselves in a difficult position if they don't promote you', wryly suggests consumer marketing expert Philip Spencer.

It is also important to recognize situations where you will never be able to 'beat' the system and therefore need to divert your energies elsewhere. The issue of organizational politics is discussed in depth in Chapter 7.

Fred Mahoney, who has spent many years managing companies in the UK and the USA, says that you should 'Analyse and identify the characteristics of the managers promoted to senior positions in the company you work for. If the company promotes commodity traders to senior positions and you are a technical manager then the chances are that you will not be promoted ... in most corporations there are glass ceilings through which you cannot pass unless you have certain characteristics.' Occasionally these characteristics may not be related in any real way to an individual's ability to do the job.

The issue of back-stabbing and acting ruthlessly was raised by one respondent, who suggested a vital strategy for moving ahead: 'The guys at the top didn't get here by being wholly good at their jobs, they have climbed there on the backs of their fallen colleagues. These guys are mostly driven people who see the world with different eyes from their normal colleagues. If you are not a driven guy don't bother entering the race! Find a senior manager who thinks you are good and let him drag you through.'

Finding a sponsor

Linking in with the above point, a number of respondents specifically mentioned that gaining promotion required sponsorship from one for more senior staff members. It is important to identify sponsors who are seeking career advancement for themselves, and then to prove to them that you can demonstrate your skills and are worthy of their support. A word of caution: when your mentor leaves, your career may go with him/her.

Other key strategies

Other successful strategies included:

▮ Having a clear notion of where you want to go, understanding your life's priorities and taking steps that allows you to move in that direction.

▮ Being prepared to study, learning from others, going on training courses, preparing for appraisal and maintaining a positive mental attitude.

Table 2.3   One senior manager's formula for getting promoted

1. Get the best out of your current job – do the hard things that show you to be different to others who may do the job in your place. Also do not stay in one job too long, I would say 3–5 years is the maximum.

2. Talk to people in different jobs to ensure you know what they entail. Find out what these jobs need and if you could make an impression by doing them. NEVER choose a job because it sounds important – you must be able to do well in it.

3. Make sure you have an end point in mind – albeit somewhat vague at a particular stage, plan out how you could get there with a few job moves. It is key to the question – 'why do you want this job?'

4. Do not be afraid to move out of your immediate comfort zone as it will stretch your capabilities. For example, doing a job you know you can do in a foreign county, or applying principles you have learnt in one business in a somewhat different business sector.

5. Tell key managers about your ambitions, ideally this will be your line manager. Talk it over with these people and look for an agreed plan and timing. Don't wait to be spotted – you may never be.

Rob Head, former Corporate Development Manager, Octel Corp.

■ Mobility, although the willingness to move geographically came up surprisingly rarely. Mobility was seen more in the sense of moving to where the heart of the action was, whether that be another country or from field to head office. A couple of respondents did link this in with opportunities, being prepared to work anywhere and with anyone.

■ It is important to develop subordinates so that you have someone ready to take over your position. That way you will never be turned down for promotion because your manager thinks you are irreplaceable.

■ Articulate your plans to others.

■ Tell your managers about your ambitions. Don't wait passively for someone to spot your talent – you may wait forever.

Q3. WHAT BEHAVIOURS AND ATTITUDES AT WORK GET STAFF PROMOTED?

The range of answers here was enormous, and they are all useful.

A number of respondents stated that the answer to the above question depended on the culture of the company, for example: 'each company has its style and the senior managers are more likely to promote individuals that seem to have the same attributes as themselves'. Others felt that there needs to be a match between you and the company's values if there is any chance of promotion: 'If you are a quiet thoughtful person working in a loud, macho environment you are unlike to be promoted since you don't fit in.' A very distinct mismatch of values and personality was cited as a strong reason why people may need to seek advancement by moving out of their present organization.

Responses have been categorized into key headings in Table 2.4.

Table 2.4 The behaviours/attitudes/approaches that get you promoted

Behaviours and acquired skills	Personality traits	Attitudes	Strategies/ Approaches
Leadership skills	Having a good level of emotional intelligence	Demonstrating a high level of commitment to the company	Being proactive
Hard work	Confidence	Being solution not problem focused	Commitment to self-development
Facilitation skills	Assertiveness/ not being afraid to express own opinions	'Can do' attitude	Ability to see the big picture (and work towards it)
Teamwork skills	Resilience	Self-belief	Objectivity
Decision making	Reliability	Enthusiasm	Knowing which battles are worth fighting
Communication skills	Ability to think and plan ahead	Integrity	Being seen as indispensable
Influencing	Risk taking	Being respected	Well connected
Listening	Independent	Willingness to make personal sacrifices	Being clear on what you want
Being an expert	Open minded	Enthusiastic	Be associated with success
Understanding and copying company style	Self-motivated	Energetic	Working organiz-ational politics

Self-marketing skills	Sense of humour	Having gravitas where appropriate	Exceeding your goals
Ideas and innovation	Consistency	Be willing to take advice about how you behave and how you work	Good knowledge base and willingness to share it
Success in your present job	Willingness to be flexible and versatile	Being well informed	Understand ing other people
Avoiding gossip	Being a conformist	Being true to yourself	Care for business

It is immediately apparent that the list in Table 2.4 contains both truisms and contradictions. Some, for example, assert that looking after number one is the key to promotion. Others suggest that it's much more about being a team player. Some stress co-operation, others competition. There is no single policy or strategy that works on its own.

Table 2.4 also shows that successful careers are built more on attitudes than on skills. The second discovery is that approaches and strategies (i.e. how you bring your skills, personality and attitudes into play) really matter.

This research is supported by those experienced in recruitment. There is often a big difference between the text that goes into a job description and the real factors that determine success in a role. A job description often focuses on tasks, skills and responsibilities (in other words, behaviours). However, ask a senior manager what *really* makes a successful post holder and the answer will usually be about attitudes and style. (This is one of the principles behind competency-based recruitment, since a competence is not only what you can do but how you do it; competencies are defined by looking at the skills, behaviours, know-how, values and attitudes of top performers). The broad lesson is that to gain promotion you need not only to possess certain qualities, but to find ways of communicating them as observed behaviours. You also need to find some way of incorporating them into active approaches and strategies.

There is clearly no single formula for gaining promotion. Since the key step is being aware of both yourself and the organization, a career development strategy will need to be flexible enough to cope with both.

Q4. WHAT SINGLE PIECE OF ADVICE YOU WOULD GIVE TO SOMEONE WHO WANTS TO ACHIEVE A PROMOTION AT WORK IN THE NEXT 12 MONTHS?

The primary responses to this question are summarized in Table 2.5.

Table 2.5 Advice for the next 12 months

- Do a good job, exceed expectations, focus on your self-development
- Have a plan of action and stick to it
- Know the business and where you can make the best visible impact
- Identify key decision makers and network
- Raise your profile
- Be flexible and realistic
- Know the way the company works (and work that way)
- Be a generalist rather than a specialist
- Persist!

Do your job well

This was the biggest category of response. However, this information must be tempered against the characteristics and actions outlined in Table 2.5. How are you going to do your job well? Who is going to notice?

Approximately 25 per cent of responses suggest in one way or another that you should put in extra effort, work towards the next level and pursue an active programme of self-development.

Rod Howgate suggests that you 'Fulfil your specified role in such a way that your managers are more than satisfied by your all round contribution and your colleagues would support your promotion.'

Bill Hollyhead offers: 'Deliver what is important to your boss. Work hard to do what you do now very well and be recognized for it. Be in the right place at the right time.' Another typical response was to our survey was: 'Demonstrate your ability to the maximum and try to perform above the level of your current post, doing more than the job requires.'

Many suggest that you should show a genuine interest in your chosen career and demonstrate dedication. HR Director Dr Ian Webb takes an analytical approach: 'Identify the next promotional job, develop a sound model of the job and the personal requirements for it. Analyse how well the job is currently being performed and thinking about the future and your own skill set develop your skills to perform; the job more effectively than it has been in the past.'

Have a plan of action

For at least 20 per cent of respondents it is considered important to be clear about what you want, have an overall game plan, and communicate it. Others add the proviso that your plan must fit in with your family and outside life.

It also seems important to ensure that your reasons for taking the next step are valid. Where does it fit into your longer term career plan? What would it add to your CV?

It seems vital that your planning is as specific as possible. Derek Osborn advises: 'First work out what exact job or role you want so that you can be very goal focused. A general wish for promotion is likely to be less successful as you will not get through the selection process without a very clear idea of why you want the promotion'.

Julia Robertson, MD of Carlisle Staffing Services, has similar advice: 'Be very clear on why you are doing this, what you will bring to the new position and how you would benefit the company in the role. Don't forget how this new position will impact on your personal life (bring loved ones on board). Be aware that a position of responsibility may be isolating and distance you from some former friends. Are you ready for this?'

Stuart McIntosh, Managing Consultant for Career Management Consultants Ltd, pushes you to ask deeper questions: 'Is the next step in your career right for you? Have you looked externally in order to benchmark? Do you have regular meetings with your boss? Do you celebrate and communicate your successes to those above you? Do you have short-, medium- and long-term goals in your career and personally?'

Know the business and know where you can make the best visible impact

Most responses under this heading suggest that you identify what the business needs, move into that area, and focus your attention only on the points where visible impact can be achieved; for example, 'define what you can do for the business, build relationship with those who can help you do what you do best, find opportunities for exposure in your areas of competence'.

Deirdre Hughes (Director, Centre for Guidance Studies at the University of Derby), writes of the importance of 'knowing the strategic and operational goals of the organization and being able to articulate how your efforts have added significant value. Being willing to analyse situations from differing perspectives and being prepared to find ways in which your line managers feel you are working "with" them rather than "against" them. Sometimes this means having to let go and helping them think through ideas to find the appropriate answers for themselves (supported by evidence, guidance and advice that you can feed into the process!).'

Identify key decision makers and network to raise your profile

Several respondents made a case for active networking, building relationships and enlisting the help of a coach or mentor. Networking is seen as most helpful with people that have influence and can make decisions, but it's important to demonstrate that you can get on with anyone you work with.

Other key points made include the need to be visible, communicate your achievements and your wish for promotion, and do something active about promotion possibilities.

Frederick Mahoney also has a practical strategy: 'Start applying for jobs inside and outside your company. You have to make it known you want to move and/or be promoted. Your boss may help you applying for all these jobs.'

Jo Bond, UK Deputy Managing Director of outplacement specialists Right Coutts, simply says 'Ask for it! Make sure that those with the power to grant your wish know that you want it!'

Be realistic and flexible

Here the voice of experience suggests that you need to be aware when you are flogging a dead horse. Knowing when your strategy isn't working is about understanding when it may be time to jump ship. Chapter 10 offers guidance on knowing when you've reached this point, and how to plan your departure carefully.

Equally, don't put a rigid time limit on gaining promotion. Jane Moorhouse believes that 'if there is nowhere for you to be promoted then work at improving your skill base'. Ron Feasey would suggest the need to be realistic about promotion: 'do you deserve it and are opportunities available?'

Be a generalist rather than a specialist

HR consultant Doreen Wright says: 'Consider where you want to be next and start to understand the processes attached to the new role – moving from specialist to more of a generalist.'

Several other respondents echoed this advice. It may not be true for all sectors, particularly those where special expertise is valued. However, as a general trend it seems true to say that becoming overspecialized can be a career block (more on Career-Limiting Actions in Chapter 9).

Other key points included persistence in sticking to your goals and implementing your strategy, and the importance of knowing the way your company works. Find out what your boss is looking for when considering promoting someone, talk their language, and be aware of the talent that is available outside the organization.

'MUST DO' LIST

☑ What one key action or event has helped you in your career? How can you repeat that step, or build on it?

☑ What strategies or approaches outlined here can help you to succeed?

☑ What behaviours/attitudes/approaches have you used effectively at work?

☑ Which do you need to develop?

☑ How are you going to build on the advice you have been given about taking action within the next 12 months? (See also Chapter 13 for further tips.)

Your DIY Career Pilot Kit

This chapter helps you to:

▌ Rethink the idea of your career

▌ Adopt a 'career awareness' strategy

▌ Check the main focus of your work

▌ Learn how to be your own career coach

▌ Conduct your own six-step career review

We do not deal much in facts when we are contemplating ourselves.

Mark Twain

WHERE YOU BEGIN

Planning for promotion success isn't just about short-term positioning, and it isn't just about getting the next rung up the ladder. It's about taking control of your career.

Having looked at how others have managed their careers in Chapter 2, we now move to active steps that you can follow. This begins with a DIY career review: becoming your own career coach.

Undertaking a personal review is one of those activities we're happy to put off, like dental flossing, or throwing out old photographs. Both analogies are useful. First of all, we need to think about how healthy our jobs are at present and what maintenance we need to do. Secondly, from time to time we need to review our past, just like pulling out the photograph album.

When a large ship approaches harbour it picks up a pilot, a trained officer who knows the local waters well. No matter how senior the captain of the ship, command shifts to an outsider during a few critical manoeuvres.

We tend to do the same thing when we want to progress in our careers. We turn to mentors, experienced friends or advisers. We put our careers in the hands of human resources departments or managers. We sit back and watch them pilot us around the breakwater and into harbour, relieved to get safely alongside.

That's the model most of us have inherited as far as job progress is concerned. We entrust it to others: we hope our line manager will notice the contribution we've made; we hope that a successful appraisal may mean that the boss keeps us in mind for a promotion. Some of these strategies may work, but they all rely too much on other people.

DIY piloting makes you master of your own ship. *You* make the critical steps, you begin to shape your future around the kind of work you find satisfying and motivating. Most importantly of all, *you* decide when, where and how.

When should you conduct your career review?

Ideally you should do some kind of career review activity every 3 months, even if this is only keeping a record of your successes and adding to your networking. Other critical times will be:

▌ when you're in a fast-moving environment and opportunities are throwing themselves at you day by day

▌ when you feel you have more to offer your organization

▌ when things are going well and you want to build on success

∎ when you feel that you've learned all there is to learn in your job

∎ when you don't find the job challenging any more

∎ when you're unhappy in your work and want to change something.

Can you really control your career? This is a question I am asked all the time by workshop delegates, and yet there is evidence all around us that DIY career management is increasingly possible and necessary. Perhaps we don't recognize when it happens.

Rethink 'career'

The whole idea of a 'career' has undergone huge changes over the last two generations. We're all familiar with the idea that none of us has a job for life. We know that it's very likely that we will have to change jobs and possibly even careers (see Chapter 12 for the results of a recent opinion poll on this topic). So we feel that we should do some 'career planning'.

The problem with the idea of a career plan is that it seems like a very demanding mix of hard work and future gazing. We all feel that we ought to have some kind of plan, and that everyone else has one. In fact, very few people have their lives planned out that precisely. Even so, we all feel guilty for not having a clear plan, and for letting our working lives be guided by chance: the job that just happens to come along. It's as if you are going to plan a holiday by picking on the first flight you find on the airport departures board. A great strategy for a spontaneous adventure, but perhaps not the best way of deciding how to spend 100,000 hours of your waking life.

Beware the idea of the perfect job

We all have bad days at work, and sometimes it's easy to feel that everyone else but you is having a great career. It's important to dispel the myth of the perfect job. The danger with the idea of a perfect job, a job that provides 100 per cent satisfaction, is that this is an ideal; the next step is to believe the perfect job probably doesn't exist, and certainly doesn't exist for *me*. When we do this, we use the idea of the perfect job to avoid getting a better job; in fact, to avoid doing anything.

Beware the counsel of perfection. For many people it justifies the status quo. It's one of the discoveries I made by writing a book entitled *How To Get A Job You'll Love* – readers are attracted by the title, but quick to shoot the idea down. *If only … Those jobs don't exist at my level … Other people get jobs they love, not me … I'm too old … I don't have the right qualifications … .*

You don't have to get the perfect job, or a job that you will love all the time. However you might like to consider an idea that you can do something about: *making your job better than it is*. The chances are that even if promotion isn't your explicit goal, this will probably happen as a result of the attention you give to role development. People take what you do more seriously when you focus on the things you do well and communicate your successes.

If you genuinely can't improve the job you're in, then career development will be about moving towards a job (or an organization, or a lifestyle) that is a much better match for you.

Career awareness

I firmly believe that the most powerful working model for the present economy is *career awareness*. Career awareness is not about having a cast-iron 20-year career plan, but having the ability rapidly to match opportunity to personal goals. For some people it will also be about the long game – the kind of role you want to hold in 5–10 years' time. For most of us, it's about being alert *now*.

Career awareness is a far more active process, and is focused on what we can do *now*. It begins with the question *'How can I fix the job I'm in?'*, moving to *'How can I get promoted?'*, and only reaches *'How can I find a better job?'* when you're fully ready. It's a strategy that doesn't depend on luck or job change, but begins with three basic questions:

▌ What kind of work do I really want to do?

▌ What does my employer really need?

▌ How can I exploit the overlap, or create one?

Career awareness avoids the pitfalls of long-term career planning and focuses on both quick wins in your present job and positioning yourself for changes that you can make in your career within the next 6–12 months. The emphasis is very much on what you have to offer now, rather than falling back on the idea that you have to retrain or go back to full-time education (again, two great reasons to put off career development).

Sandy was temping for a major UK organization concerned with culture and the arts. She originally took the job just to do secretarial work, but gradually discovered that the organization has many overlaps with her personal areas of interest: culture, languages, foreign travel and project management.

Even as a temp she has been allowed to benefit from company training programmes. Having enlisted the support of her line manager, Sandy has taken every opportunity she can to meet people from different departments of the organization, to discover what roles are available and to undertake suitable training. She has also reaffirmed her project management and team skills, and currently presents a positive message that will make her a highly suitable candidate when permanent vacancies occur within the organization.

What kind of awareness is involved? Awareness of you, how others see you (see more about personality later in this chapter), what your present or next employer is really looking for, and an understanding of the way in which work is changing.

What is your focus?

I spent some time in early 2003 looking at the employment situation in the Bay Area of California. Pegi Wheatley, owner of McCall Staff Services in San Francisco, told me that as most people now have reasonably strong IT skills, managers focus more than ever on personality. Pegi has been placing executive secretaries in San Francisco for over 28 years, and says 'I see top secretaries in two ways: as *process* people or *project* people.' In other words, some successful post holders need to be mainly focused on the nitty gritty of a process (vital if you have a boss who's big on promises and weak on detail); others are great at initiating and managing projects, often handling several at the same time. Here detail is still important, but the main ability is to demonstrate enthusiasm and commitment to new ideas.

In a world where technical skills are taken more for granted, there is increasingly more attention on interpersonal skills and how you use them. The business environment changes very rapidly, and highly valued staff don't just need to ride the wave of change, they need to keep ahead of it. This means keeping a focus on two areas: what you have to offer, and the experiences you seek in the future.

Being focused means knowing what you're good at and being able to communicate that to decision makers: your present boss, other managers in the organization, and not forgetting representatives of outside organizations, including customers.

Your career focus needs to be about *how* you handle this week's problems and how far others are aware of your results. If multitasking and managing complex problems come easily, perhaps your contribution is undervalued because you don't value your skills and accomplishments. It's important that people who will have a say in your future have a sense of what you *really* do: the times when you have snatched victory from the jaws of defeat, the times when a calming influence rescued a key account, or a clear head made a key event run smoothly.

Your contribution matters to the bottom line of your business and to the peace of mind of your boss. But be aware that your duties include a responsibility to yourself to make sure that the way you execute your role is appreciated.

The benefits of DIY career piloting

Time to take your first tentative steps towards coaching yourself towards success. Becoming the pilot of your own future has a number of benefits:

▮ Awareness: you become more aware of what you have to offer, and how to communicate your message to your employer, colleagues and customers.

▮ Wish List: you are able to form a concrete wish list of what you want to get out of work, which leads to:

▮ Goals: clear, coherent goals, with a clear starting point (see Chapter 5).

▮ Positioning: you become more aware of how you are placed in relation to colleagues, clients and decision makers.

▮ Influence: you begin to see how you can make a difference or add value.

▮ Power: how much leverage do you have to change the situation you are in? It's important here to distinguish between the leverage you think you have, and your actual power over the future.

You begin to learn:

▮ how to tell the difference between what you can fix, and what you can't

▌ how to obtain and exert leverage

▌ how being in the right place at the right time is no coincidence

▌ how to manage your luck

▌ how to make decisions, rather than be subject to them

▌ how to recruit others to help you along the way.

DIY CAREER REVIEW

A   Diagnose your constraints

B   Formulate your goals and message

C   Identify your skills and achievements

D   Realize your intellectual capital

E   Understand the way your personality fits into work

F   Examine your attitudes and values.

A. Constraints: the barriers between you and success

In Chapter 1 you had an opportunity to conduct an audit of your job satisfaction. That's the first step. Look at the positives and negatives in your job, and take a positive look at both. How can you improve the good parts of the job? How can you diminish, delegate or avoid the uninspiring parts?

Most people don't find it difficult to list the problems in their jobs. However, as soon as the conversation turns to fixing them, they become highly creative at coming up with reasons why nothing can be done. Being a DIY coach is about really asking how far you are limited by external constraints, and how far internal blocks are getting in the way. Table 3.1 shows examples of both.

Table 3.1 Constraints

External constraints	Internal constraints
Can you get round them? If not, what's the best career strategy to work with them?	Look at how far these prevent you from changing anything. Where have you overcome these problems in the past?
I need to work near home	I'm underqualified
I need to avoid a long commute	I'm too old
I want to live near where I work	I am no good at networking
I don't want to move house	I'm frightened of making the wrong move
I need £xxxx a month minimum	I'm not good at pushing myself forward
I have health problems or a disability	I hate being rejected
I have personal or family commitments	I'm frightened of losing my job

As Table 3.1 reveals, we do have genuine constraints, but the most powerful ones are usually internal ones: the kind of inner message that wakes you up at 2 o'clock in the morning. These have a powerful effect on your *world view*, your picture of how life operates. Dealing with these constraints is vital as the first step in your DIY career review.

B. Goals and message: where do you want to be?

Chapter 4 tells you more about distinguishing goals from dreams. Work out the things that are real goals.

With a goal in mind, you can build up a clear, coherent picture that combines your preferred skills, your intended pathways and the kind of work you want to do. Your message may be communicated either verbally or in writing, but should be something that you can condense into one sentence: *'I want my job to allow me to do A, B and C so that I (and my employer) can achieve X, Y and Z'.*

Without making people feel bored or threatened, it's perfectly possible to let colleagues and managers know your message. Just be sure that you offer it as a solution, not as a complaint (see Chapter 6 for tips on offering a win/win solution).

You may like to give some thought to the question of when and how you communicate your message. With some people it will have an immediate impact and effect if you communicate verbally. You may then want to reinforce what you have said with an email or a memo.

Ken is an associate with a specialist firm of consultants who advise businesses on cost reductions. He's felt stuck in his career for several years and dissatisfied with his job. However, in the past 12 months he has received two promotions. He had two turning points: one was to really look at his strengths, his achievements, and to realize that he had far more to offer than his company was using. He drew up a strong CV and developed a wish list of what he wanted to do next. The second change was a new boss. Instead of assuming the same kind of relationship with his new boss, Ken made a positive career pilot decision. He offered his new boss expertise and advice about getting the team to work better. He bought new suits and shirts. He put forward a range of initiatives that would present his boss 'quick wins' and look good. Now Ken gets taken along to the kind of meetings that only staff four rungs above him attend. Having a change of boss can sometimes mean that you can reposition yourself very astutely.

Others take more time to respond and don't accept new information readily. With this kind of manager or colleague it's often best to prime the pump by warning them that a piece of communication is on its way and then send something in writing. Indicate when you would like a follow-up discussion.

Think about what you may need to add to your message. Extroverts want to hear passion, logical people want to hear reasoning. Others want to see evidence, hear the benefits (what's in it for me?), or maybe want to see how what you suggest fits into the big picture. Look at the communication strategies outlined in Chapter 6.

C. Know your skills inside out

The real key to getting your message straight is understanding what you are good at. This may seem perfectly obvious, but most managers will tell you that few of their staff are fully aware of their skill set, and fewer still are capable of communicating them, for example in an appraisal interview. Secondly, we're able to complain about the skills we are not allowed to use, but not so good at negotiating chances to exercise or improve them.

Chapter 10 provides a range of short cuts to skill identification.

D. Realize your intellectual capital

If you were only allowed to make a living from what you *know*, how would you set out your stall? Put another way, what specialist know-how, understanding or information do you have that makes you a key contributor to your organization?

Cataloguing your areas of knowledge

▪ Times when colleagues seek you out for your specialist knowledge.

■ Areas of research, analysis or surveys you have undertaken.

■ Topics on which you have written reports for internal use.

■ Topics on which you have written articles.

■ Subjects in which you have trained others, or spoken about at staff seminars.

■ Areas of knowledge to which only a few individuals have access.

Extending your areas of knowledge

■ Seek parallels from other industries or sectors.

■ Find out how others achieve success and ask for their tips on shortcuts and minefields.

■ Find out as much as you can about the work of others; become a fount of knowledge on who does what.

■ Keep a cuttings file or resource book to record useful resources and contacts.

Showcasing your areas of knowledge

■ Collect and distribute useful information.

■ Ask to be given the chance to produce surveys of best practice, specialist techniques or resources.

■ Contribute to in-house or industry journals.

■ Be known as an information broker, a great source of data and connections.

E. Personality fit

If you want to move up in the organization, it pays to have an understanding of the way in which you relate to cultures and teams.

Find an opportunity to undertake some personality testing. It's a self-reporting measure, so you won't get any nasty surprises. What you should get is some helpful feedback about the way you react, typically, in a variety of situations, how you respond to change, new ideas, other people, and in teams. With some measures you will be given feedback around what psychologists call the 'big five' personality traits. One measure, Quintax, has been produced by Stuart Robertson & Associates in Manchester, UK (see www.sr-associates.com). Quintax's five-fold structure is outlined below as an example of the kind of feedback that you will receive from a well-developed personality measure.

1. **Extroversion**: this tells us if you are more at home in the outer world of people and things, or in the inner world of ideas and reflection.

2. **Criticality**: this tells us whether you base your judgements more on impersonal logic and analysis or on personal values and feelings.

3. **Organization**: this concerns whether you like a decided and orderly way of dealing with life, or a more flexible spontaneous approach.

4. **Intellectual focus**: this is about whether you like to think about possibilities and relationships among ideas, or deal practically with known facts.

5. **Emotional involvement**: this is about whether you feel and express your emotions in reaction to events, or whether you tend to contain your reactions to things.

Each of these elements can help you to unlock the way your personality best integrates with different workplace situations. For example:

1. **Extroverts** tend to do well in action-oriented environments, particularly where there are people to influence, manage or control. **Introverts** tend to be less impulsive and more prepared to consider and reflect before acting.

2. The degree of **criticality** you bring to work will often indicate the kinds of tasks and organizational cultures that suit you best. If you are strongly driven by logic, then systems and processes will often have high appeal. Those with low criticality tend to be

more influenced by the feelings of others, and very much in tune with why relationships succeed or fail.

3. All work requires a degree of **organization**, but some people are more comfortable with structure and timetables, while others like to keep life flexible and possibly even enjoy interruptions to the routine of life.

4. Your **intellectual focus** reveals whether you are a grounded, pragmatic kind of person, or whether you like to think about underlying theories. Are you the sort of person that says 'if it ain't broke, don't fix it', or the kind who is keen to try out new ideas in the workplace?

5. Your **emotional involvement** will often be a good indicator of how you cope with criticism in the workplace, and how you cope with rejection when your 'offer' isn't accepted. On the plus side, those with high scores in this area tend to be energized and passionate about the work they do.

F. Examine your attitudes and values

We all take our values to work with us. Your **values** are expressed in work through the tasks and outcomes you find interesting and meaningful. Sometimes this is on a macroscale: you're interested in what your company makes and how it contributes to the world. For others values are expressed in relationships at work and the way in which staff are treated.

Values are closely related to motivation. We throw ourselves into tasks not just because they are interesting, but because they fit our career drivers. For more insights into what motivates you at work, see Chapter 4.

The survey in Chapter 2 also revealed the power of the right **attitude** at work. Think about what you feel, and what you show. If you are more introverted than others, you will tend not to display your feelings. Sometimes, if you're also a fairly theoretical person, you will sit and listen to ideas without communicating very much. These are elements that matter when it comes to attitude: what you show is more important than what you feel. If you have people around you who need to *hear* and *see* encouragement, make sure they do so.

In today's work environment, attitude is often focused on the way you feel about change. The important question is *how do others believe that you feel about change*? Business gurus often tell us that the most important driver in a business is the willingness of staff to commit to change. You don't have to be a deep-down enthusiast for a change-a-minute workplace, but resistance to change may well be a Career-Limiting Action (see Chapter 11).

Marketing recruiter Linda Clark says: 'Be reasonably conformist – which demonstrates that you fit in – while at the same time show that you add real value to the organization.'

Top career strategists are careful not to invent a new wheel; they learn from others. Part of the way forward is to identify successful career pilots and find out how they did it, and how they have learned to 'read' their boss, their marketplace and their employer's needs, which is where we go in Chapter 4.

'MUST DO' LIST

- ☑ Look at how far your career to date has been limited by your own dominant picture of what a 'career' is, and how it's supposed to work.

- ☑ Explore the options available to you if you think outside these rules.

- ☑ Work through your DIY career review. Getting others to help will add to your insights.

- ☑ Find out more about your personality. How well do you work in the kind of team you are in? How well do your working style and preferences match those of your boss and colleagues?

What Do You Mean By Success?

This chapter helps you to:

❚ Look at success in your terms

❚ Find out what really motivates you

❚ Set and achieve real goals

❚ Understand your career drivers

❚ Begin to renegotiate elements of your job

Chance favours the prepared mind.

Louis Pasteur

I WANT TO BE SUCCESSFUL

Being successful in your career means different things to different people. In the broadest terms, it means receiving some kind of external validation of what we have achieved. In the past this was usually measured by money or status, but we live in a society where the relationship between people and work is complex. We want more out of work, and different kinds of validation. Men and women often 'read' careers quite differently. We seek rewards in different ways at different times of our lives.

We may define our idea of career success in a number of ways:

■ I want to be recognized for the skills I have to offer.

■ I want to be able to provide for my family.

■ I want to be happy at work.

■ I want to make a difference.

■ I want to be well paid.

■ I want to be in a senior position in an organization.

■ I want to run my own show.

■ I want to develop a national or international reputation.

■ I want to have control over my life.

■ I want to make things happen.

■ I want to work with people who share my values.

■ I want to win.

UNDERSTANDING WHAT MOTIVATES *YOU*

It's likely that your picture of what you want to get out of your career has changed at least a little during the course of your working life. When we get our first job we tend to focus on the surface aspects of work: receiving a pay cheque, having a job title, fitting into an organization. Later on we start to think about what work is really about.

Our career drivers are the psychological factors that prompt us to want to work, and the reasons we want to work.

EXERCISE 4.1 – THE 3-MINUTE MOTIVATION CHECKLIST

What motivates you to get up in the morning and go to work? Look at Table 4.1. Imagine that you have £20 to spend on yourself, and you can spread that £20 on any or all of the things that really motivate you in work, taken from the list below. You can allocate £20 to one motivator, or spread it among as many as you like.

Table 4.1 The 3-Minute Motivation Checklist

Motivating factor	£££s
1 **Status** My worth is recognized in my job title/paylevel/car/responsibilities …	
2 **Recognition** I am recognized for my skills and contribution	
3 **Feedback** I know when I am doing a good job	
4 **Skills balance** My opportunities and skills are well matched	
5 **Challenge** I like to take on new projects and problems	
6 **Success** I enjoy being a winner	
7 **Personal development** I have continuing opportunities to learn and stretch myself	
8 **Variety** My work is varied and interesting	
9 **Responsibility** I am responsible for important things/people/projects	
10 **Company values** I recognize and agree with the values of my employer	
11 **Independence/freedom** I have some control over how I spend my time at work and where I go	

Continued

Table 4.1 (Contd)

Motivating Factor	£££s
12 **Fun** I am totally absorbed in what I do	
13 **Team membership** I enjoy being part of an active, supportive team	
14 **Making a difference/contributing** I can see what my contribution adds to the whole process	
15 **Helping others** My work contributes to others, or to society as a whole	
16 **Meaning and fulfilment** I find my work meaningful and fulfilling	
17 **Security** Knowing what I will be doing and earning in a year's time matters to me	
18 **Earnings now** I am relatively well paid in comparison with my peers	
19 **Earnings potential** My earnings will probably increase significantly in the future	
20 **Fringe benefits** The job has interesting perks	

Look at where you have allocated your scores in Table 4.1. Imagine now that you are in a job and the money issues are resolved. You are being paid what you feel you deserve, and you have reasonable prospects of pay increases in the future. If you have allocated any score to the bottom three rows, boxes 18–20, now reallocate these £££s to any other motivators on the list.

Money and motivation

Why do we consider and then sidestep the issue of money? Because money is for most people a weak motivator. I regularly run workshops for sales staff, and ask them to imagine that it is mid-December and they have just been awarded a 10 per cent pay increase with effect from 1 January. How long, I ask, will the pay rise motivate them to perform better? Usually the answer varies from 2 to 4 weeks. We all get a thrill when the pay comes through in our first pay slip, but after that a pay rise has very little impact on performance.

Now turn the situation around. Imagine it's mid-December and your boss says 'It's been a rough year, and sadly I am going to have to ask you to take a 10 per cent pay cut from January onwards'. How long do you think that a pay cut has a *negative* effect on performance? Most workshop participants usually say 'until I get a new job'.

Note, however, that there is a small part of the population who are capable of constantly remotivating themselves around financial targets. Often they do this by competing against themselves, constantly resetting the stopwatch and chasing new targets. If you have someone like that making money for you, hang on to them!

In 1910 a London newspaper ran the following advertisement:

> WANTED: volunteers for a hazardous journey. Small wages. Bitter cold. Long months of complete darkness. Safe return doubtful. Honour and recognition in case of success.

There were 10,000 applications for 20 positions on Shackleton's expedition to the South Pole. Who says that money is life's main motivator?

Focusing on your motivators

Look again at the list of potential motivators in Table 4.1. What will really encourage you to give more at work? How do you like to receive external validation? Do you get enough feedback, praise or encouragement? Perhaps what really motivates you is enjoying being part of a team, or learning new things. If so, does your present role provide what you are looking for? The reality is that we can do very little of this validation for ourselves. We need external feedback: praise, encouragement, reward, benefits.

The 3-Minute Motivation Checklist only provides a rough sketch of your career drivers. You need to turn to a more detailed breakdown: see Exercise 4.2 at the end of this chapter.

Issues such as money and working conditions have a relatively small positive impact for most of us, but a huge negative one. In other words, putting someone into a bright clean office won't guarantee a better performance, but moving someone into a dark, dingy environment almost certainly will result in worse performance.

Money dominates the issue of motivation, partly, I think, because it's the easiest thing to talk about. If a friend asks you why you want to move job, or what you want out of a career move, it's simple and easy to say 'more money'. Probe behind that answer and you usually get to the true motivators – the buttons an employer needs to press in order to get you to act more enthusiastically, to go the extra mile. These are also the factors that will ultimately persuade you to stay in a job or move on: what an organization needs to do to retain you.

Why do we misunderstand motivation?

It's interesting to compare the way that employers and their staff perceive motivation. The issue of motivation has been studied from the perspective of both employees and managers. In one study, by Thomas Crane and Lerissa Patrick (*The Heart of Coaching: Using Transformational Coaching to Create a High-Performance Culture*, 2002), managers were asked to guess what motivated their workforce. Employees ranked as numbers 1 and

2, respectively, 'Appreciation' and 'Feeling "in" on things'. Managers tended to overestimate the importance of money, estimating that this would be the top motivator, followed by job security. Workers tend to emphasize less tangible motivators such as appreciation and being 'in the loop', and for many people there are very specific motivators that have nothing to do with money, such as the ability to learn new things, or a pleasant working environment and courteous people.

One interesting question is: why do managers forget what it is like to be an employee as soon as they are promoted? Almost inevitably managers feel that they have to deal with money and promotion issues because that's what they spend most of their time talking about when they are negotiating around job content. This is useful to know, because it is often far easier for your boss to improve the non-financial aspects of your job. Ultimately it's your job, and your manager's job, to increase the number of motivators in your work, and decrease the things that turn you off. If your organization won't fix them, it's up to you.

How might your company say thank you?

Work is a deal. You offer your time and energy and commitment, and an employer provides you with a range of benefits and opportunities in return. The range of things an employer can offer is perhaps broader than you think. Some of the items on the following list will in fact cost your employer very little. Remember, the elements you negotiate should be related to your primary motivators, as explored in Table 4.1.

Rewards/opportunities you may try to negotiate

▮ Increased flexibility, e.g. flexitime, or finishing early one day a week.

▮ Learning opportunities (funding, supporting or encouraging courses you do, whether undertaken in working hours or not).

▌ Work shadowing and job rotation to increase your work awareness and skill level.

▌ Opportunities to initiate and manage new projects.

You can discover more about negotiating different aspects of your job in Chapter 9. One of the ways of looking at this issue is to think of your job as a series of commitment zones, as set out in Table 4.2.

Table 4.2 Commitment zones

Time	Your perspective	Employer's perspective
30–50% Core zone	Some of this may be routine, but it needs to be done, and failure to complete this work will give you difficulties with your boss.	Covers the basic elements of the role. The job gets done; you're a safe pair of hands.
30–50% Push zone	Time where your employer may be pushing you outside the obvious remit of the job, asking you to go the extra mile, bring extra enthusiasm and commitment.	Your willingness to respond, within reasonable limits, influences the picture your employer has of you.
5–10% Exploration zone	Your personal playpen: opportunities to try out new roles and ideas and explore career possibilities.	You will usually have to persuade your employer to give you this freedom, and communicate the benefits before and after you do it.

Looking at commitment zones is helpful because it focuses on expectations: yours and your employer's. We look at this trade-off in much more detail in Chapter 5. Other chapters discuss ways in which you can use your 'exploration zone' to expand the boundaries of your job, and Chapter 12 looks at ways of using this time to explore new career possibilities.

SETTING REAL GOALS

Goals and dreams

As soon as you begin to look at your commitment to the job, you see that you need to focus on activities that matter. Setting real goals is about sorting out the difference between fantasy and reality. We all have daydreams; sometimes they are an important distraction from routine and dull activities. You may dream of living in a beach hut in the West Indies, or running a second-hand bookshop in New York, or winning Formula 1. Daydreams are a necessary entertainment. But one of the things we like about them is the fact that we do not have to actually do anything about the daydream. It is a pure, self-enclosed fantasy.

Goals are rather different. There is no point having a goal unless you are prepared to explore ways of achieving it. Indeed, many would say that there is no point having goals unless you are prepared to *do* something about them.

A goal is something you can move towards. You can clearly see that there is a series of footsteps between you and a real goal. It's possible to imagine and plan the step just before you achieve your goal, and the step before that. Once you begin to visualize those footsteps you are forced to come to the conclusion that there is a step right in front of you. For most of us taking that step requires a conversation: finding something out, seeking out someone who has already achieved or discovered something, recruiting a mentor or coach. The powerful thing about the next-step principle is that you have to discover a powerful reason not to take it, and it's much harder to resist one step than several.

Begin with your daydreams, with blue-sky thinking. What would you really like to do? Where would you like to get within your organization? It's widely recognized that the first, critical step is to define your goals and write them down. Here are the other critical steps, set out in reverse order from the point of goal achievement and working backwards to the first action.

Steps to goal setting

8. **Begin with the end in mind**. Imagine how you will feel just after you have achieved your goal. If your ambition is to give a public address, imagine the moment after you have finished a successful talk. Anticipate the feelings that will come immediately after you have achieved your goal.

7. **Look at the outcome**. How outlandish/unrealistic/outside your comfort zone is this goal? How will you feel if you are retired and you haven't got there, or never tried?

6. **Look at the last steps**. Imagine the final steps you have to take. The last moments before reaching the top of the mountain. The moment you are called on stage to accept your award. The day you put your key in the door of your own business.

5. **Look at the intermediate steps**. What will you have to do on the way? What will you need to learn?

4. **Look at the barriers**. Imagine looking back at life from a time when you have achieved your goal. Look at the time between now and your goal as if it was history. What were the greatest obstacles? What kind of knockbacks did you get? Who tried to put you off your goals? How did you deal with rejection and criticism?

3. **What are the first steps**? If your goal is going to become reality, what do you need to do in the next 6 months? Remember to give yourself incentives for each step, and recruit people to do some encouraging.

2. **What is your first step**? What do you need to do right away? Who do you need to speak to? Where do you put your first footstep?

1. **Why do you want to change**? Look at where you are now and **step 8**, where you want to be. What happens if you do nothing?

EXERCISE 4.2 – YOUR CAREER DRIVERS

What do you really want to get out of work? Complete Table 4.3 to work out your detailed career drivers.

Table 4.3 Your career drivers

Code	Put a cross here if you actively want to AVOID this	Write your score in this column: 3: Essential 2: Very important 1: Of some importance 0: Not important or irrelevant
S Stability Staying in one job for a while		
S Security Being able to plan financially		
S Large organization A 'steady' employer		
S Stated goals Clear targets and objectives		
S Routine Predictable daily workload		
		TOTAL S SCORE:

Table 4.3　(Contd)

Code		Put a cross here if you actively want to AVOID this	Write your score in this column: 3: Essential 2: Very important 1: Of some importance 0: Not important or irrelevant
A	Working alone In my own time and space		
A	Directing my own work, Not being micro-managed		
A	Power to decide Authority to make key decisions		
A	Time freedom Controlling my diary, setting my own deadlines		
A	Independence Doing things my way in my time		
			TOTAL **A** SCORE:

Table 4.3 (Contd)

Code		Put a cross here if you actively want to AVOID this	Write your score in this column: 3: Essential 2: Very important 1: Of some importance 0: Not important or irrelevant
P	Helping society As a whole, or one community		
P	Building community Putting something back in		
P	Serving others Putting my skills at the service of those with the greatest need		
P	Making a difference Making a personal contribution to an issue or problem		
P	Helping the environment A job that is environmentally conscious or friendly		
			TOTAL **P** SCORE:

Table 4.3 (Contd)

Code		Put a cross here if you actively want to AVOID this	Write your score in this column: 3: Essential 2: Very important 1: Of some importance 0: Not important or irrelevant
E	Building something from scratch Creating something new		
E	Making money For myself and others		
E	Launching new ideas New products or services		
E	Running my own show My own unit or my own business		
E	Excitement The buzz of activity or challenge		
			TOTAL **E** SCORE:

Table 4.3   (Contd)

Code		Put a cross here if you actively want to AVOID this	Write your score in this column: 3: Essential 2: Very important 1: Of some importance 0: Not important or irrelevant	TOTAL M SCORE:
M	Influencing progress Taking things in the right direction			
M	Mastering change Coping with rapid change			
M	Rapid pace Enjoying life in the fast lane			
M	Targets Need a new challenge every day			
M	Continuous improvement Believing there's always a better way			

Table 4.3 (Contd)

Code		Put a cross here if you actively want to AVOID this	Write your score in this column: 3: Essential 2: Very important 1: Of some importance 0: Not important or irrelevant
C	Champion innovation Promoting new thinking		
C	Thinking outside the box Using lateral thinking		
C	Invention Coming up with new concepts		
C	Being artistic Doing this artistically, with a sense of balance and design		
C	New angle Seeing things afresh, having a new take on things		
			TOTAL **C** SCORE:

Table 4.3   (Contd)

Code		Put a cross here if you actively want to **AVOID** this	Write your score in this column: **3: Essential** **2: Very important** **1: Of some importance** **0: Not important or irrelevant**
L	Family Work that is good for family life		
L	Time balance Leaving time and energy after work		
L	Commuting and travel Limiting the time I spend travelling to or from work		
L	Well-being Time and space to be healthier		
L	Location Working at the right distance from home		TOTAL **L** SCORE:

Table 4.3   (Contd)

Code		Put a cross here if you actively want to AVOID this	Write your score in this column: 3: Essential 2: Very important 1: Of some importance 0: Not important or irrelevant
D	Influencing people Changing hearts and minds		
D	Influencing decisions Being 'in the loop'		
D	Driving people and systems Getting the best out of people and systems		
D	Leading people Leading from the front		
D	Competition Keeping a competitive edge		
			TOTAL **D** SCORE:

Table 4.3 (Contd)

Code		Put a cross here if you actively want to AVOID this	Write your score in this column: 3: Essential 2: Very important 1: Of some importance 0: Not important or irrelevant
X	Being an expert in my specialism		
X	Being consulted for my expertise		
X	Specialist knowledge Being an information broker or specialist		
X	Problem solving Trouble-shooting, relying on my knowledge		
X	Setting standards in my industry or specialism		
			TOTAL **X** SCORE:

Table 4.3 (Contd)

Code		Put a cross here if you actively want to AVOID this	Write your score in this column: 3: Essential 2: Very important 1: Of some importance 0: Not important or irrelevant
R	Recognition Being noticed for what I do		
R	Salary increments A clear ladder to better pay		
R	Standard of living Others can see I am doing well		
R	High financial rewards Earning as much as I can		
R	Reputation Being highly regarded by others		
			TOTAL **R** SCORE:

Table 4.3 (Contd)

Code	Put a cross here if you actively want to AVOID this	Write your score in this column: 3: Essential 2: Very important 1: Of some importance 0: Not important or irrelevant	
I Relationships Building up good relationships at work			
I Teamwork Being a player in a great team			
I Encouraging Getting the best out of others			
I Building people A 'learning organization', a development culture			
I Caring for people Believing that people matter		TOTAL I SCORE:	

How to interpret your results

Add up the scores you have for each code and insert them in Table 4.4 to establish your main driver types. Then identify your top 5 in an approximate rank order. Don't worry if you have equal scores: everyone is a mix of different kinds of motivation.

Table 4.4 Career driver types

Code	Driver type	Score	Rank order
S	Stability and security		
A	Autonomy: doing things on your own, or your way		
P	Purpose and Meaning		
E	Enterprise and action		
M	Change master: driving change, and thriving on it		
C	Creativity		
L	Life/work balance		
D	Drive/influence		
X	Expertise/specialisms		
R	Reward and recognition		
I	Interaction with people		

EXERCISE 4.3 – SETTING GOALS FOCUSED ON YOUR CAREER DRIVERS

1. Refer back to Table 4.3. Look at the individual items you gave a score of 3.

2. Decide on your top 10 and list them in Table 4.5 as your top 10 career drivers. In the right-hand column, give yourself a score out of 5 judging how far each driver is met in your present role.

3. How closely does this top 10 relate to your choices in the 3 minute motivation checklist (Exercise 4.1)?

Table 4.5 Your top 10 career drivers

My top 10 career drivers	How far is this driver met by your present job? (5 fully, 3 moderately, 1 not at all)

How could you do your job differently to increase the scores in column 2? What goals can you now set yourself to begin the process of changing your job?

'MUST DO' LIST: BUILDING ON YOUR MOTIVATORS

☑ What really motivates you? At work? Outside work? Work out the factors that really do encourage long-term commitment. As far as work is concerned, what motivates you to get out of bed on a winter morning?

☑ If you were your boss, what would you have to do to retain you? Think about the ways you would like your job to grow and change.

☑ What is the best way for your employer to reward you? Once the money issues are resolved (and especially if they are not) how do you like to be thanked? Think of what you would really find encouraging and helpful.

☑ Which commitment zones do you work in for most of the time? Are you signalling your contribution in the 'push zone'? Are you experimenting with at least a small proportion of your time?

Solving Employers' Problems: The Key to Promotion Success

This chapter helps you to:

▋ Check how much you know about your organization

▋ Begin to see work from an employer's perspective

▋ Identify Key Result Areas

▋ Perceive what identifies you as useful

▋ Focus on outcomes as well as objectives

▋ Manage your time to achieve the right results

There is nothing so useless as doing efficiently that which should not be done at all.

Peter Drucker

THE BIG PICTURE

In Chapter 4 we looked at what makes you work effectively. Where are you going to direct that energy? Here we look at ways of matching up what you do best to the needs of your employer.

Too many careers go off-line because staff focus on the wrong kind of picture. If you are looking just at the microlevel (your job, your department, local problems and opportunities) you may be achieving great results, but you may not be creating the kind of evidence that will get you promoted, simply because one of the primary things you need to contribute is the way that your job contributes to the organization as a whole.

In this chapter we are going to focus on the critical areas that will enable to you to focus on solving employers' problems:

▍ focusing on Key Result Areas

▍ understanding the organizational perspective

▍ working effectively, and with more focus

▍ using time management to create more 'wins'.

Getting promoted is often about getting noticed, and to do that you need to contribute to the big picture. Coaching specialist Stuart Carter reflected in our survey on the three steps that had presented him as being more in tune with organizational objectives: '(1) Ensure that personal achievements contribute strongly to the company strategy and targets. (2) Learn, digest and focus on the key items you need to deliver on – if you have targets understand clearly what actions you need to take that will have the maximum influence on those targets. (3) Don't be afraid of blowing your own trumpet.'

Key Result Areas

The chances are that your job description contains a great deal of information about duties and responsibilities, but only limited information about Key Result Areas (KRAs). This is one of the ways in which employers measure your performance in a job (but not the only one; see 'Outcomes sometimes beat objectives', below). Many respondents to our survey indicated that career success is about really understanding what an employer's main problems and opportunities are about: what your employer really needs.

KRAs are useful because they provide a benchmark for success. Firstly, this applies to your own role within the organization. Whether you are negotiating a new role or discussing a job you've done for some time, the questions in Table 5.1 will be helpful both to you and to your manager.

Table 5.1 Questions around Key Result Areas

1 **What is the purpose of the job?**
Why is this job here at all? What headache, problem or opportunity does it address?

2 **What does the job contribute?**
What leverage does this job exert?

3 **How does the job fit into the organization?**
How does my work depend on/impact upon others?

4 **What specific skills or knowledge are required?**
What else do I need to learn to be successful? Who is available who already has these skills or knowledge?

5 **What are the main problems to be solved?**
What can go wrong? What skills will I need to fix problems? How did previous post holders survive?

6 **How much freedom is there to act or make decisions?**
How much space do I have to use my initiative?

7 **What controls or limits apply to the job?**
What are the budgetary, organizational or time constraints?

8 **What quick wins are expected and possible?**
What results need to be achieved quickly, and how will they be measured?

9 **What results does the job exist to achieve? How is performance measured?**
What are the long-term outcomes? How will they be measured? Who will judge what is meant by success?

10 **Who needs to be influenced to achieve a result?**
Who will support the outcome, and who will get in the way?

11 **How should the result be communicated?**
Who does the outcome need to be communicated to? How?

As Table 5.1 makes clear, there are many questions to be asked to ensure success. Don't make the mistake of thinking it's just about hard work.

How aware are you of your employer's needs?

Table 5.2 offers you a chance to work out how in tune you are with the key facts about your present employer.

Table 5.2   How much do you know about your employer?

Key questions	Very aware	Moder-ately aware	I need to discover things fairly quickly
Who are the top decision makers in your organization?			
Who is likely to retire within the next 2 years?			
Who is likely to be promoted to a key position within the next 2 years?			
How did your company begin? What are its origins?			
What is your company's Mission Statement?			
What is your company's best/worst-selling product or service?			
How profitable is your company compared to others in its market sector?			

Table 5.2 (Contd)

Key questions	Very aware	Moder- ately aware	I need to discover things fairly quickly
How has the share price of your company performed compared to its closest competitors?			
What is your company's most/least profitable activity?			
Who is your company's biggest customer?			
Who is your company's biggest competitor?			
What is your organization's market share?			
What are your company's strongest brand values?			
What differentiates your company from its closest competitors?			
What trade or professional associations have strong links with your company?			
What major new products or services are likely to come on line in the next 12 months?			
What new products or services from competitors are likely to impact on your company?			

Continued

Table 5.2   (Contd)

Key questions	Very aware	Moder- ately aware	I need to discover things fairly quickly
What new legislation is coming along that may affect your company or your job?			
What is your company's track record for staff retention, recruitment and training?			
Who makes most of the decisions about staff development and training in your organization?			
Who else in your company performs a similar role to you in a different department or division?			
What does your company say about itself in its brochures/ magazines/handouts/website?			
What picture does the press have of your company's reputation and values?			
Who are the key people who know the answers to most of the above questions: people you need to speak to within the next month?			

OBJECTIVES AND REAL RESULTS

Focus on objectives

Most management courses tell you about setting and achieving objectives. These are important: it's about deciding what you mean by success, and working out how and when you can say you have got there.

Your job may have explicit objectives. These may be expressed on a functional level (e.g. to check and process 100 application forms) or may be linked to quality standards (e.g. achieving above-average customer satisfaction ratings). The best kinds of objective are *measurable* (so you know when you've hit them) and *planned* (you know what you have to do to reach them). Better still, objectives should be related to the bigger picture: where your organization is going.

Workers who are given information about the way their role contributes to the bottom line usually contribute more. They see their small effort contributing to something much bigger than their job.

The very best kinds of objectives are also linked to motivation. We all know about setting SMART objectives (Specific, Measurable, Achievable, Realistic and Timebound). This covers the basics of good objective setting. But do you really feel like getting out of bed on a cold winter's morning to fulfil objectives that are simply specific, measurable, achievable ... ? Possibly not. We actually need to work to objectives that are also motivating and rewarding. For more on the power of motivation, see Chapter 4.

Outcomes sometimes beat objectives

You are already aware that career awareness is about changing things in a short timescale, and looking at quick wins. Firstly, let's agree one principle: businesses are built around perceptions, not just facts.

If you look at published research on customer relationships, most surveys tell you that the reason a customer leaves you isn't because of poor quality, your prices, your technical ability or delivery times. In most surveys 60 per cent of customers say that they switched to another supplier largely because they felt they weren't being looked after.

Think about buying a meal in a restaurant. An objective-driven approach to getting your meal in front of you will focus on measurable standards: food temperature, quality, visual presentation, time from order to service, and so on. However, what really matters is that we walk out of the restaurant feeling that we had a good experience. That's probably going to be less to do with conformity to someone else's standards, and more about feeling that we were made to feel welcome and slightly special by the restaurant staff. In that atmosphere all food tastes better. Customer loyalty to brands and services is more about feelings than facts. We know what we like.

This has important implications for your career, especially if you have always believed that success is about activity and targets, about measurable objectives. These are noted, but don't set the world on fire. Objective setting is an important building block in business, but the most successful businesses (and the most successful workers) also have an instinctive understanding that outcomes can be more powerful than objectives.

To take a business example, a departmental meeting will have objectives (getting through the agenda, commissioning new projects, allocating workloads, seeking ideas or information, etc.). However, a meeting will also have important *outcomes*; for example, whether people get on better with each other, whether the meeting ends with clear goals, and whether people are more informed, more motivated, more committed than they were at the outset. You could say that outcomes are part of the hidden agenda, and this is sometimes more important than the explicit agenda. With some teams, for example, being able to work together is just as important as what they are working on.

Most services are complex, and if we try to measure them just in terms of objectives we miss the main issue: how do people *feel* as a result? You may run a meeting at work strictly by company rules or good management principles, but what if you can create a better outcome by breaking the rules, or by not holding the meeting at all?

People tick objectives but remember outcomes.

Working to real results means focusing on what really matters at work. If what's critical is that your boss looks good or feels reassured, then work towards that outcome. This will often be about how you work as well as what you achieve. If your boss likes you to do something in a particular way, it's often best to work with the grain rather than against it. If your boss has a particular hobby horse (wants you to be in work before her in the morning, hates surprises, wants you to remember people's names, or likes you to have a perfectly tidy desk), achieving that outcome may be more powerful than anything else in your job description. Watch particularly for pet hates. If, for example, your boss hates you to dress informally even on dress-down days, this could be the kind of permanent irritant that gets in the way of promotion.

ALIGNING YOURSELF WITH THE ORGANIZATION

Think the way employers think

If you have ever heard the way that managers criticize their subordinates, often it's along the lines that X 'isn't on board' or Y 'doesn't get it'. An important reason for friction and a potential block on promotion prospects is a mismatch between the way you think and the way your employer thinks.

This doesn't require a brain transplant, but rather your ability to tune up your radar. Look at the language that is used by your organization. Are you in tune with this year's buzzwords? Your ability to use these terms in an intelligent way indicates your success in really thinking about the major concerns, problems and opportunities of your organization.

For Bill Walmsley, Business Development Director of CERTT, success was about 'recognizing that organizations (invariably) behave according to an often unwritten cultural code – presenting business cases in a manner consistent with the code is essential in gaining support for career enhancing initiatives.'

Sometimes the key to success is being able to think like your boss (or your boss's boss) thinks. If you can begin to do that, you have a far greater chance to begin to communicate in a way that your boss will find meaningful. This isn't simply about buzzwords, but about focusing on what your boss finds important. Getting promoted may simply be about working out your boss's biggest headache, and solving the problem. If the problem can't be solved, it can at least be tackled. The main thing is that your boss sees that you are playing by the same rules and with the same objectives in mind.

Careers coach Rob Stickland suggests: 'Pinpoint an organizational need about which you have strong positive feelings then focus your energy and time on that issue so that you become expert in it. When you know what you're talking about start your own personal PR campaign aimed at fulfilling that organizational need.'

Match the language

A small tip is to become aware of the language that key people in your organization use. What is the dominant set of metaphors? Whether your company is into 'roadmaps' or 'cutting-edge thinking' or 'empowerment', it often helps to begin to match your language with the kind of language used by key players. Done with some subtlety and understanding, this goes a long way to communicating the fact that you are sensitive to your employer's KRAs.

Use the 10 per cent principle

The 10 per cent principle is an interesting business model that has powerful implications for career-enhancing activities. The principle is this. If you want to set up a new business in your local area, for example a sandwich shop, you don't hunt around for a high street where there are no other sandwich shops. You find one where there is a busy sandwich shop. There is already a clientele, already a flow of business, and nobody needs persuading that buying a freshly made sandwich is a good idea. What you do in order to compete is to do something using the 10 per cent principle. To succeed you only need to be 10 per cent *something*: 10 per cent cheaper, 10 per cent better quality, 10 per cent faster, or have 10 per cent more choice of sandwich fillings.

How can you use this principle in your job? Think of your employer as your customer, and others around you as suppliers. Look at what others do which is seen as effective and exciting. What can you do 10 per cent better, or faster, or more creatively? However, the difference is that in an organization this approach will work far better if used in co-operation rather than competitively: if someone is doing something successfully, ask whether you can join in and bring your ideas to the party. However, if you are comparing your offer with someone outside the organization, such as a supplier, you may have a very strong offer on your hands: something that can be done more cheaply and to a higher standard by bringing it in house.

Early warning system

Look at some of the major problems around you at work at the moment. How much easier would they have been to fix when they were minor problems? Perhaps you have a problem with a supplier who is underperforming and delivering late. What were the early warning signs that there was going to be a problem? Hindsight has 20/20 vision, so surely it's better to put in place some kind of early warning system?

The early warning system would wreck most disaster movies. Someone would notice the smouldering wires in the skyscraper, or the airline pilot's early symptoms of food poisoning. When warned not to approach Dracula's castle, the young couple in the forest would turn around and find a B&B. If you can spot the small signals that indicate trouble ahead, you've discovered a quick win, and something that gets you noticed. Don't overdo it, though, or you may be seen as a prophet of doom.

Sometimes spotting future problems has the powerful effect of preventing your boss from being caught napping. One respondent to our survey, Peter Bell, suggested: 'Always ensuring your superiors are never surprised by events or results helps to ensure their confidence in their position and in you. There are some setbacks that are unavoidable; if superiors are prepared they are seen to be on top of things and therefore confident in your abilities.'

BEING CLEAR ABOUT THE STARTING POINT

SWOT your situation

Many people come across SWOT analysis in training, but don't see how it's a brilliant tool for spotting an employer's problems and seeing how your employer thinks. Use it to look at your own department, unit or team. Begin with the everyday information that is readily available to you and your colleagues: the way you work, your biggest customers, your biggest headaches. You might take the initiative and suggest using a SWOT analysis as a discussion focus for a team meeting.

A SWOT analysis (see Figure 5.1) looks at the strengths and weaknesses of an organization or team. This is a way of looking at the present situation; so what happens if nothing changes? At this stage you are focused on internal factors, and remember to look at all of the strengths of your situation: your colleagues, your resources, your client base. Strengths usually means focusing on the skills and expertise in a team, while

Figure 5.1 SWOT analysis

weaknesses will often be about gaps in service or understaffing. It may also be about weak administration or bureaucratic obstacles.

How can the results help you to get ahead? Because career progression is most commonly achieved by a combination of self-awareness and insight into the reality of your employer's situation, you may be the first one at your level in the organization to wake up and smell the coffee.

The upper half of the SWOT diagram looks at *internal factors*, both positive and negative. **Strengths** will probably include key staff, retained knowledge and expertise, and may include other factors such as brand strengths and market position. **Weaknesses** often arise because it's difficult to hang on to any of these strengths: people leave, and know-how becomes stale or out of date.

The lower half of the SWOT diagram looks at *external factors*, and also looks at *future* possibilities. What opportunities have already presented themselves that you have yet to exploit? What threats can you perceive?

This exercise works well on a small-scale level because you are often able to do something with the results. It is an extremely useful tool when you are trying to identify KRAs, because these will inevitably feature in the SWOT picture. You may be concerned about what you do when you discover negatives: what do you do with this information? Remember that you will contribute directly to KRAs by spotting early warning signals (see above) and generating positive behaviours that result in quick wins.

Using SWOT to highlight critical areas

The most sophisticated use of a SWOT analysis, however, relates to strengths. A company can be very smug about strengths, so the most revealing (and disturbing) question sequence is 'What is your greatest, unique strength? And what is the *weakness inside that strength*?' For example, a company's greatest strength may be the brand values of its top-selling product. How easily can those values be imitated by competitors? How long will the brand maintain its position in the marketplace?

The analogy with your own career position is that you may take your strengths too much for granted. If your strength is your good relationship with a key manager, what happens if that manager moves on? If your strength is your technical ability, what happens if a consultant offers your company an even higher skill level? If your strength is your knowledge, how up to date is it? Figure 5.2 shows an example of a SWOT analysis applied to one individual's position within a company.

Quick wins

Once you've got an idea of what you need to do to help your company, and how you need to do it, you need to get some quick wins. A quick win is not a motivational gimmick, but a practical

STRENGTHS	WEAKNESSES
• My client list	• Lack of time to attend industry conferences
• My sales skills	
• My contacts within the company	• Long hours on the road mean I don't spend time with key managers in my company
	• My Divisional Manager doesn't know me very well
WEAKNESS INSIDE THE NO. 1 STRENGTH	
	ACTION: Schedule meeting with Divisional Manager to share my success
• My clients could easily be reallocated to another consultant	
OPPORTUNITIES	**THREATS**
• Spinning out new business from existing clients	• External competitors
	• Rising stars in my own company
• Looking after my clients and checking service levels more personally to reduce the weakness inside my main strength	• Divisional Manager wants to make cost (staff?) cuts
	ACTION: Learn from the most successful pitches and products of competitors
ACTION: Focus on building client relationships	

Figure 5.2   A SWOT approach to an individual career

reality: what is the most successful activity you can undertake in the shortest time, with the minimum of effort and resources?

New managers going into companies often miss quick wins. They want to put huge strategic changes into effect. These take time and often meet resistance. Others know better. The best way is to walk around and talk to people about the work they do. Ask them for things that can be fixed quickly. Often people on the shopfloor know exactly what's going wrong. They will identify 'just this one small thing' that gets in the way; and it's usually about doing something very simply and immediately improving either efficiency or customer satisfaction.

You can do the same in your job, either from your own observation or from what people say around you. But remember, quick wins need to be chosen carefully, because they must be prompt and they must be successful. See Chapter 11 for more tips on quick wins.

Matching personal excellence with your employer's wish list

Your path to promotion is about knowing the best version of yourself and how you can be at your best.

Understanding how your employer thinks is a vital part of the process, because then you can begin a dialogue between your personal goals and the organization's key result areas: in short, gaining promotion and career satisfaction while your employer achieves the right outcomes. Penny Chester, Managing Consultant for Right Coutts, believes that what matters is 'commitment in the face of difficult or demanding circumstances, running the extra mile, integrity when organizational politics beckon, sound knowledge base and generosity in sharing it'; in other words, a focused application of individual skills and values to a particular work context.

It's up to you. One of the things about being a grown-up at work is that you are the only one, ultimately, who will take charge of your future. Pursuing personal excellence is about identifying the kind of working life you would find most motivating, rewarding, challenging and inspiring. Translating that into promotion is about working out, step by step, how your personal excellence matches up to an employer's thinking and solves an employer's problems.

You get where you want to be by ensuring that your employer, the most important customer in your life, experiences a real sense of achievement: the organization has gained something important by having you around.

'Lots of companies are going through structural change at the moment', says Linda Clark, Senior Partner in an executive search consultancy. 'Try to find out where the organization is focused and set yourself up to be in the team which is going to be the centre of the strategy. Join up for something nobody else wants to do. If it has to be done, you may get the job and a promotion at the same time. Join a team of well-respected individuals. If they are going places, you can go with them.'

KEEPING TIME ON YOUR SIDE

In order to manage your workload, you need to manage your time, even if it's just about creating the time to research and deliver quick wins.

You've probably been on training programmes that promise to improve your performance through time management. Very few of them really impact upon performance in real terms.

In my experience the principle that has maximum results is the 80/20 model, otherwise known as the Pareto principle. It's fascinating how frequently this principle applies to work and society. In most countries, for example, 80 per cent of wealth and resources are owned by 20 per cent of the population. In work, 20 per cent of your time produces 80 per cent of your results, as shown in Figure 5.3. The flipside of this is that 80 per cent of our time is unproductive, gaining only 20 per cent of our results.

When you're thinking about contributing to your employer's KRAs, this really matters, if only because it's likely that only 20 per cent of your efforts at work will build up your reputation and your promotion prospects. Working out what exactly that effort constitutes, and how to protect that vital time, is vital.

Your visible, effective and most noticed productivity is achieved in just one-fifth of your working time. The problem is

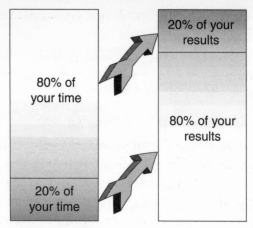

Figure 5.3   The 80/20 principle

that if you lose any of this 'win time' to distractions, your results tail off dramatically.

How do you find your 'win time'? Look backwards, from the results. Look at the most important objectives you achieve, and the most significant outcomes. What do you do in order to achieve them? What exactly do you do in that time? What gets in the way? Let's say that 8 hours a week achieve the greatest impact. If you allow this productive time to be cut in half, that has a huge leverage on your final results.

The first and critical step in time management is to work out exactly what you are doing in your 'win time' and to protect that time as far as you can. If possible, extend it slightly. The first step with this is to look at all of the things you do that are almost entirely unproductive. Cutting these activities back by as little as 30 minutes a week can create a huge impact on your end results.

In short:

■ Losing half of your 20 per cent 'win time' can mean losing 40 per cent of your contribution to KRAs.

■ Protect your 20 per cent 'win time' carefully against time stealers (see below).

▌ Do everything you can to attract 20 per cent activities and delegate or avoid 80 per cent activities.

▌ Persuade your boss to delegate to your strengths, not your weaknesses, and you will probably operate more securely in the 20 per cent zone.

▌ Try to expand your 'win time', if only by a small margin.

The solution? Work out the what, exactly, you are doing when you are most productive. Ring-fence that 'win time' to ensure (1) that you are interrupted only by tasks or problems that meet *key* objectives (e.g. a call from an unhappy and important customer) and (2) that this time is not eaten away by time stealers (Table 5.3).

Table 5.3 Typical time stealers

▌ Allowing staff to bring you low-level problems that they can deal with unassisted

▌ Answering queries that someone else can answer

▌ Colleagues or subordinates trying to delegate to you

▌ Overlapping responsibilities

▌ Reinventing the wheel

▌ Doing everything yourself and failing to delegate

▌ Working to contradictory or fuzzy expectations

▌ Being unclear in your instructions

▌ Delegating responsibility but not authority

▌ Allowing preferred tasks to distract from key activities

▌ Failing to plan, so that everything is unexpected

▌ Attending or calling unnecessary meetings

▌ Fatigue

▌ Junk mail (paper and electronic)

▌ Failure to set a procedure for handling routine matters

▌ Gossip and informal chat

▌ Fighting fires, and never taking the time to focus on true KRAs

'MUST DO' LIST

☑ Work out the Key Result Areas in your job, your team, and your company.

☑ Where have you become too focused on objectives and missed the real outcomes?

☑ Agree your personal objectives with your line manager, then reflect on the outcomes that will be equally powerful.

☑ What early warning signals can you spot now that may prevent or limit problems ahead?

☑ What quick wins can you identify and deliver within the next 6 weeks?

☑ What activities really contribute to your 'win time'?

☑ Hunt down your main time stealers, and protect your 'win time'.

Marketing Yourself Within the Organization

This chapter helps you to:

▋ Market yourself to your employer

▋ Work out how others see you

▋ Communicate reasons why your employer should keep you on

▋ Manage one-to-one and team encounters that move you on and up

▋ Make effective, memorable presentations

Competition brings out the best in products and the worst in people.

David Sarnoff

IT'S ALL ABOUT COMMUNICATION

How disposable an asset are you?

As we saw in Chapter 5, getting promoted isn't about what you do, it's about employers noticing what you do. Skills alone are not enough.

Think of yourself as a corporate asset: a building, a piece of equipment, a vehicle. Disturbing, isn't it? Suddenly you feel much more disposable. Companies boast that their people are their greatest asset. At times it seems that people are their greatest *disposable* asset. Why do we dispose of things? Because we feel we no longer have a use for them. We get rid of equipment, vehicles, buildings, even information, when:

1. we haven't used them for a while

2. they don't contribute directly to success

3. they're a headache

4. we can't remember why we got them in the first place.

Staff can be made redundant for a huge variety of reasons. Often it's about major reorganization, or about a rapid change in the marketplace. If that's the reality, there's little you can do about it except learn how to move on positively. However, it's also true that companies use external reasons (e.g. the marketplace, restructuring, new systems) to dispose of human assets. And while there are logical, surface reasons for getting rid of particular people or departments, the staff that companies tend to get rid of first fit the four categories listed above.

So communicating your strengths within an organization isn't just about getting promoted. Sometimes it's about keeping your job. And it's always about being seen to be about making a direct and visible contribution, being seen as an asset.

I don't feel comfortable with promoting myself

It's perfectly reasonable to have some hesitation about self-promotion. You begin by looking at the real purpose of the activity. Is it about you, or about the organization?

Self-promotion that is merely about *me*, about projecting my ego. We're really telling the world how important we are. Sometimes saying '*I'm the best thing since sliced bread*' gets your audience's attention, but it's important not to believe all your own PR!

Not everyone is self-obsessed. Look at the way top career performers market themselves rather than simply indulging in self-promotion.

Marketing as a discipline presents some useful parallels. True marketing isn't obsessed with the qualities and features of the product, but focuses on the needs of the buyer. It asks 'what do you need?' rather than asserting 'this is what we are selling'. Empty self-promotion is like unfocused selling, a hard sell that pushes something you don't really need or want. Empty self-promoters are like those dreadful telesales people who ring to sell you double glazing just as you're sitting down to supper. They have very little idea of what you need, or what will interest you; they just want to get through their sales script. Self-promotion only has one focus: *me*, not the outside world. Self-promoters spend more time talking than listening. They enjoy the sound of their own voice and they enjoy the limelight. If they are interested in people's reactions, it's because they are interested in seeing a reflection of their own glory. The world is full of people who want to sell, but very few true marketeers.

In our survey, Business Link executive Helen Rodway gave the advice: 'Be seen but don't be too opinionated, argumentative or verbose'.

Talking to others is a critical step. Jane Moorhouse, previously a senior executive with the NAAFI organization, suggests that you: 'Only share known facts with your team and don't gossip. Walk the floor and know everyone and their roles, don't force team building; listen.'

Those who are skilled at marketing themselves to organizations are determined to communicate a match between what they have to offer and what the organization needs. Their message is not *look at me,* but *I can offer something which will help* (see Table 6.1).

Table 6.1 When self-promotion doesn't work

Self-promotion behaviours	Marketing behaviours
I tell	I listen, then tell
I am focused on, or even obsessed with, me	I am interested in my influence on the organization
I compete	I co-operate
I seek opportunities to win at the expense of others	I seek opportunities to find win/win with the organization
I promise the earth, then underperfom or perform a vanishing act	I underpromise and overdeliver
I exploit weaknesses	I build on strengths
I speak this week's buzzwords	I am in tune with my organization's anxieties and ambitions
I put spin on the facts	I present facts credibly and carry conviction
I convince people in the short term	I give people long-term evidence of my reliability
I move onwards and upwards	I make a lasting contribution and maintain relationships with former colleagues, bosses and teams
I exploit other people	I enable others to work more effectively

Self-marketing: a more positive approach

You may hate self-promoters and have a real reluctance to blow your own trumpet. But it's important to distinguish between self-promotion, which is ego-driven, and the need we all have to market ourselves to organizations. True marketing focuses on the needs of the customer, and that's what successful workers do: work out their employer's biggest problems and greatest opportunities, and then communicate a match between what they have to offer and what the organization needs. Your career really gets on track when you find a trade-off between your goals and the current anxieties and vision of your employer.

Self-marketers spend more time listening than talking. They discover. They listen to what people need. They pick up the right language, and become sensitive to the concerns and hopes of the organization. Most of all, they have a sense of perspective: the big picture. Whether your forte is managing the details or kick-starting the next project, always try to have a sense of how this contributes to the business in the widest sense; and if you don't know, find out.

Don't self-promoters sometimes succeed?

Sometimes the worst kind of self-promotion works, even when it's driven by vanity, narcissism and a Machiavellian lust for power. It's also true that the worst kind of sales techniques (pushy, insensitive, manipulative) work, and so do the worst kind of management techniques (coercive, bullying, overbearing). It's equally true that fraud, deception and mugging old ladies can create an income stream. These methods get results, but often not in the long term, and always at a cost: to the person behaving in this way and to those on the receiving end.

So a word of warning: be aware that others will be competing around you who are true self-promoters. They will use every trick in the book: ego-massaging, manipulation, half-truths and lies. It's all to easy to acquiesce to this kind of behaviour or, worse still, to believe that this is the only behaviour that will get you success in your organization.

I've heard a number of clients say *I don't want to be promoted – I've seen what you have to become.* First of all, you have to question whether their colleagues really became something different, or whether they simply changed their behaviours. Secondly, you have to challenge the idea that there is only one kind of person who will succeed in your organization. Look at the full range of senior figures in business life, and you'll find a wide range of personality types and a wide range of personal values. You can find ethical, sensitive, highly spiritual people at the highest levels (just as you can find mean-minded, bitter and self-obsessed people at every level in an organization). Three things, however, come out in most surveys of business leaders: they have the ability to deal with people, the ability to have a strong vision and work towards it, and sufficient personal strength to remain themselves throughout the ups and downs of the process.

If you are genuinely worried that the price to be paid for promotion is unacceptable, this needs exploring. Is it a genuine fear of negative characteristics in you that will be emphasized or exploited? If you have a tendency to cut corners or bend the truth, will you become really lazy or dishonest? Or is there something about the way you *read* the organization that makes you believe that you will have to behave in unacceptable ways?

The cost of ascending the slippery pole

Real career progression shouldn't be about the damage you do to other people in order to get to the top. If it is, life has a habit of biting you back. Shark-like behaviour works in the short term, but leaves you short of friends. It also does huge long-term damage to organizations, work colleagues and personal relationships.

Success should be about standing on the shoulders of giants, not clambering over others in a mad scramble to the top. If you have any lingering doubts about the balance of ethics and results, take the long view. How many of the people who backstab their way to the top have long-term friendships outside work or relationships of trust in work? How many of them could go back to one of the organizations or people in their past and ask for help? It's unlikely that any of us will lie on our deathbed wishing we'd made more enemies.

WORKING OUT HOW OTHERS SEE YOU

Seen and unseen

When considering the impact you have on others, and how far you are able to communicate your strengths to an organization, it's important to know your limitations and enlist the support of others. In marketing terms it's the difference between a new product that you think is a marvellous idea and something that is tested among target purchasers.

The Johari window (Figure 6.1) provides some insights into the difference between the way we see ourselves and the way others see us.

	KNOWN TO MYSELF	UNKNOWN TO MYSELF
KNOWN TO OTHERS	**1 OPEN SELF** Aspects of yourself that you are aware of that are also perceived by others (the impression you know you are giving)	**2 BLIND SELF** Aspects of yourself that you are NOT aware of that are perceived by others (the impression you may be giving, unknown to yourself)
UNKNOWN TO OTHERS	**3 HIDDEN SELF** Aspects of yourself that you are aware of that are NOT perceived by others (the part of you that you hide)	**4 UNKNOWN SELF** Aspects of yourself that you are NOT aware of that are NOT perceived by others (unexplored aspects, hidden strengths and motivations)

Figure 6.1 The Johari window

The idea behind the Johari window is that we achieve personal growth by expanding area number 1. We can only discover information in boxes 2 and 3 in relationship; by listening to others (2) and by disclosing to others (3). We can only reach box 4 by reflection, and again this often works best when supported by others.

This tool is useful because it shows that employers and work colleagues may be making decisions about you based on information in (2): attributes that are perceived by others, but not by you. You need to know whether this is the case; this is one of the major benefits of feedback and appraisal, discovering exactly how others see you and how that relates to your self-image.

You may discover that many of your strengths are hidden away in box (3): you are aware of them, but others are not. This is the importance of self-disclosure, which in commercial terms comes back to the key issue: marketing yourself.

THE SPECIFIC SKILLS OF SELF-MARKETING

As we have discovered, communicating yourself within an organization is essentially a piece of marketing, one that is most effective if you have a strong grasp of how you are seen already and how you would like to change that perception. The following checklist rehearses different contexts for active marketing.

Reaching out to people

Successful workers are often those who have cultivated a wide range of contacts within the organization as information resources. You need a team of people who can assist you on your journey:

∎ trusted colleagues who can advise you on the way you are perceived by the organization

▌ honest friends who can tell you about the way you look and sound (don't ignore surface essentials such as dressing well, looking smart, sounding alert, writing and speaking without making major grammatical mistakes)

▌ contacts within the organization who can tell you the real agenda and the most desired outcomes

▌ those in your company who know the key people: whom to talk to, who can tell you what's going on

▌ others who have access to key information and knowledge

▌ colleagues with particular skills from whom you can learn

▌ other successful performers: what can you learn from their behaviours?

▌ the key people you need to influence and impress.

Formal one-to-one meetings with senior managers

Think carefully about one-to-one encounters with anyone who is a key decision maker. Chapter 9 talks about the way you should use contact time with your boss very carefully. If you have the opportunity to discuss something or communicate information to someone even more senior, use that time even more imaginatively.

Remember that this may be the first time that this senior manager has heard your voice or seen what you can do. Up to now you may have just been a face or a name. The first impression you make here will be as important as the initial impact you may make in a job interview, except that here the stakes could be even higher.

Think carefully about why you are there. Is it to ask a question, to convey information or to put forward an idea? Are you looking for a view or a decision? If your role here is essentially *input*, plan what you are going to say and go through it briefly and concisely. Back up your spoken words with written information. Be prepared to answer questions, but don't let them put you off communicating your main message. If you are seeking *output* from a senior manager, make it very clear from the outset what you are looking for: 'I'd like your view about ...' or 'I wonder if you can give me a decision on ... ?'

Some warnings and reminders are:

- Make sure *your* boss is aware of the conversation beforehand if he or she might feel threatened or sidestepped by this conversation.

- Be clear what you want to get out of the interaction.

- Don't ask for information that you could have obtained from this manager's subordinate or, worse, from a document that is already on your PC.

- Confirm details in writing, if necessary in a follow-up email or memo.

- Always fulfil, or overfulfil, anything you commit to during this meeting. If you don't, the manager will assume that you are unreliable in all aspects of your work performance.

Other one-to-one opportunities

You may discover many informal opportunities to interact with key decision makers in your organization; suddenly discovering that the head of finance is next to you in the lunch queue, for example. You may bump into a senior member of staff in a social situation. You may be working side by side (possibly in roles of equal status) in a voluntary assignment.

When this happens, don't assume that this manager will remember who you are and where you work. A reasonable good way is to say hello warmly, and quickly introduce yourself by name and function. What next? Be careful of anything that impinges on personal matters (even your director's choice of dessert!), but perhaps say something positive about her most recent press appearance, conference speech or article in the company newsletter. Don't let flattery become fawning, but it never harms to show that you are aware of someone's profile.

The principle here is about putting yourself on the map and increasing the awareness of key people. But tread carefully.

Should you engineer such an encounter? This is very much a matter for personal style, both yours, and that of the manager you are trying to meet. There have been successful approaches made through encounters that weren't quite chance, such as knowing when someone is likely to take coffee or emerge from a lift. Keep it natural and relaxed; as soon as what you do looks calculated or obvious, or becomes repetitive, the greater the chances of your contact having the opposite effect to the one intended.

Your contribution to teams

Your contribution to teams gets noticed, both by people in those teams and by those who hear reports of team activities.

A general principle here is to keep cynicism under wraps. It's all too easy to accept the prevailing tone when others are running the company down, or, worse, criticizing key figures. Join in, and you never know how your words will be repeated. This could be another Career-Limiting Action.

Positive and negative behaviours in teams are most effective when they are new teams that mix staff from different departments. You're on stage in much the same way that you will be when you make a public presentation (see below). If your contribution is positive and effective, it's highly likely that news of this will reach key decision makers.

Chapter 10 will give you the opportunity to identify your natural team role and seek opportunities (particularly in cross-departmental teams or teams involving key players) to join and work with teams. Seek teams that form to undertake a particular project and then disband when the project is complete.

Committees, in contrast, have a life of their own and can tie you down to unproductive activity for years.

Relationships outside the organization

Chapter 9 gives you a great many tips on networking with key people outside the organization. What needs to be said here is that there are people outside the organization that you can influence to change the way in which your company sees you. These will include the contacts listed in Table 6.2.

Table 6.2   Key marketing relationships outside the organization

---

- **Customers**: being seen as the key link person into your organization. Customers buy people as much as products.

- **Suppliers**: being given the opportunity to achieve Key Result Areas by ensuring you attract the right resources at the right price.

- It's sometimes no harm to your career if **competitors** see your strengths; at least it gives your company a strong reason to retain you.

- Other **business relationships**: seek opportunities to represent your organization with trade associations, your local Business Link, local government and schools.

- The local **community**: being seen as a representative or spokesperson for a company is usually role-enhancing.

- **Recruiters** and **headhunters**: getting the odd enquiry or invitation to move on can be confidence building, and can also give you the opportunity to keep your ear to the ground about what's going on.

PRESENTATIONS TO INTERNAL OR EXTERNAL AUDIENCES

One of the most important means you have of influencing others is through the opportunities you have to make presentations.

This is such an important topic that the rest of this chapter is devoted to it. Why is it important? Because, as we discuss elsewhere, the decision to promote you is often made around just two or three of your actions, and what is often remembered is the time when you did something in the public gaze. You could say that being good at making presentations isn't in itself a great benchmark for being promotable, but the experience of many who make promotion decisions suggests that it's one obvious way that makes you visible and interesting, so it's the kind of event that will come up in conversations about your future.

Outplacement consultant Bernard Pearce found that this skill was critical in his own development: 'Learn to present information, ideas and concepts in a way that raises confidence and both motivates and inspires the listener! It is the ability to present well that separates the leaders from managers!'

The art of stunning presentations

Whether you're presenting to clients or colleagues, you need to know what you're doing. A good presentation to customers counts because everything you do and the way you do it is taken as an indication of supply standards.

Don't make the mistake of thinking that presentations to colleagues and superiors are any less important. In career terms, they matter first. Someone in that room may be making a decision about your next move just as you are speaking. Again, your presentation style and standard will, quite unreasonably, be taken as an indication of your total effectiveness within the organization.

Preparation

There is no such thing as enough presentation. Only the most experienced presenters can plan to 'wing it' on the day.

We watch consummate performers who appear to do everything off the cuff, and make the mistake of believing that it's all spontaneous. It isn't. Inspiration draws on experience and practice. The late comic genius Tommy Cooper's hallmark was an act that was a shambles and always on the edge of chaos. Every stumbling moment was carefully rehearsed.

US Defense Secretary Colin Powell made a critical presentation to the United Nations in February 2003. Not only did he rehearse, write and research his speech painstakingly, he delivered it several times in advance to colleagues. At one stage he had a room set up to replicate exactly the room where he would be speaking. Preparation makes the difference.

Planning to be successful

The key to success in presentations is beginning with the end in mind. Why are you presenting? What do you want to happen as a result of your talk? Do you need to make a presentation at all? There's nothing worse than listening to a 90-minute explanation of information that could be covered in a 10-line handout or email.

Getting inside the audience's head

Too much of presenting is about talking and telling. Top-performing salespeople know that the best strategy is to ask rather than tell. Ask people what their concerns are, or the gaps in their understanding. Find out before you stand up and speak.

Running the success movie

If you are nervous about presenting, here's a trick for stage fright taught to opera singers. Don't think about the initial moments of terror as you begin, but think about the final moment just after you finish: a happy, interested audience giving you positive feedback. Then work backwards, visualizing your closing moments, then the substance of what you do, and finally get to the starting point in your head.

The reason this works is that the human brain finds it difficult to distinguish between actual and imagined experience. Sports stars know this well: if you have a strong picture of hitting the finishing tape first, your brain reacts as if this is something you have actually done before, and seeks resources to help you do it again. If you visualize the best version of yourself making a presentation and practise to reinforce effective skills, then by running the internal 'success movie' you will capture some of the same results as actually doing it.

Top and tail

Memorize your opening words so that you know you will begin well. First impressions count, so don't cough, mumble or stumble over your first words. Stand straight, deliver your opening statement clearly and not too quickly – your audience is tuning in to your voice gradually and taking in a lot of other visual information about you, your dress style, your behaviours – so take it slowly and steadily. Look at people while you talk to them. Get a feeling for the mood and level of attention of the room. Memorizing a brief, strong closing statement works too. That way you know that if you get lost somewhere in the middle, you always have the lifeline of a great finish.

Design your material so that you can cut it down if you end up with a shorter time than you planned, or if you are losing the audience's attention. They may have been bored by the last speaker!

Filling the sandwich

The best presentations are short, sweet and memorable. A politician only needs 4 minutes in a radio spot to get across the three main points of the day. Most people are only capable of holding about five pieces of information in their heads simultaneously, and prefer three. If you overinform, you clutter and confuse. Begin by deciding what three key messages you want to get across.

If you have complex supporting information such as statistics or examples, use them sparingly. If you have detailed handouts, don't give them out until you have communicated your main points, otherwise half of your audience will be reading, not listening.

Beware the old adage repeated so often in books about public speaking: *tell them what you're going to tell them, tell them, tell them you've told them*. It's really dull. Be clear, and reinforce your point, but please don't say the same thing three times. Your audience is much smarter than you think.

Use humour carefully, but use it if you dare. Make your word pictures as interesting as your visuals. And make sure that you finish on a clear, positive note.

A 10-point presentation checklist

1. Stand up and walk to the lectern or end of the boardroom table as if you already have the audience's complete attention, and you will.

2. Try to have an opening statement or statistic that really catches your audience's attention. A phrase like 'Most advertising is a waste of time' usually does the trick.

3. Avoid reading from extensive notes. Use bulleted words or phrases if you need to. Often all you need is about six to 10 cartoon images in front of you to remember the key elements in your talk.

4. Use visual aids to complement what you say, not repeat it. Put only a small amount of text in slides.

5. Use more than just visual images. Physical props make great visual aids.

6. Vary your volume, tone and speed. Listen to professional speakers, and learn.

7. Look people in the eye when you tell them the important stuff. If you don't they won't believe you.

8. If you are quoting something short and powerful, pause, and repeat it.

9. Remember that 80 per cent of your message is in the way you dress and move, and in all the mannerisms and tics that distract your listener.

10 Strike the right balance between snappy and good value. You can always offer to expand at the end of your talk: if your audience wants to hear more, they will ask questions.

'MUST DO' LIST

☑ How are you communicating the fact that you are an asset and not just a cost to your employer?

☑ What style is right for you: self-promotion or self-marketing?

☑ How do others see you in the organization? Take soundings from friends and colleagues. Don't seek flattery, but an honest answer to the question 'What do people think that I contribute?'

☑ Seek opportunities to present your message to key individuals and groups.

☑ Work on your presentation style. Your next public presentation could be the deal-breaker for promotion.

Survive and Thrive

CHAPTER

7

This chapter helps you to:

▮ Move on beyond survivor mentality

▮ Learn how to avoid redundancy

▮ Move from 'survive' to 'thrive' mode

▮ Recognize the importance of 'political' awareness in a job

▮ Fit work into your life in a more balanced way

By working faithfully eight hours a day, you may eventually get to be a boss and work twelve hours a day.

Robert Frost

MOVING FROM 'SURVIVE' TO 'THRIVE'

Having looked at some of the behaviours that market you to your organization, we now look in more detail at what prevents people achieving progress in difficult work situations; in other words, why those who would like to develop their careers often fail to do so.

Understanding survivor mentality

In her thoughtful book *Strike A New Career Deal*, Carole Pemberton recounts how workers who have managed to survive waves of redundancies and downsizing become focused on job security and lose sight of both their own personal goals and the aims of the organization. The survivor mindset is to keep your head down and keep your job. Ironically, it encourages behaviours that fail to endear you to managers: invisibility, conformity, an aversion to risk taking. Carole Pemberton and Peter Herriott researched this group of workers and found that their reactions fell into four broad categories:

1. Getting ahead – continuing to seek career progression;

2. Getting 'safe' – protecting job security, seeing things out until retirement;

3. Getting out – which often involves jumping ship without any real thought or preparation; and

4. Getting even – undermining change or actively sabotaging projects in the company.

(From *Strike A New Career Deal*, Carole Pemberton,
Financial Times/Prentice Hall, 1998)

If you feel you are a survivor clinging to the wreckage, you feel you have few choices, and you feel negative about yourself and the opportunities available to you. Organizations often make the mistake of thinking that people who survive redundancy will feel so grateful to be retained that they will work harder. This is generally far from the truth. Demotivation and insecurity usually follow, along with a sense of guilt because we've kept our jobs while others haven't.

You can also find the survivor mindset in people who follow 'getting safe' thinking – keeping your head down, keeping out of the way of trouble. This might be a strategy that can work for you in the short term, but it's no way to live your working life. This behaviour almost guarantees that you are considered part of the dead wood of the organization.

Avoiding redundancy

Chapter 6 focused on the need to ensure that you're not seen as a disposable asset. You might think that it's impossible for anyone to avoid redundancy; it's something that just happens as a result of external factors. Some factors, largely external, are outside your control; some factors you can influence. The sign of a mature worker is often the ability to tell the difference between the two.

It's true that highly skilled, useful people are made redundant by organizations. However, managers will also tell you that, unofficially, organizations get rid of people who aren't part of the main event, or at least don't give the impression that they are: people whose skills seem out of date, whose contribution to the organization seems lightweight, and people who just don't fit. Anything you can do to improve your profile in a positive way is an action that does something, no matter how small, to keep you off the redundancy list.

Do be aware, however, that being made redundant shouldn't be taken, in itself, as a reflection of your employability. Organizations 'let people go' for a wide variety of reasons, and don't always get rid of the right people. So, although it's important to have a strategy to present yourself as being as useful as possible to an organization, do also recognize that redundancy is a fact of life for a large proportion of workers, and if it happens to you then don't make the mistake of taking it personally.

However, it would be very negative just to stay in survival mode, grimly hanging on to your job. How much more positive to find ways of moving from safety to achievement? One of the ways of retaining your job is to act as positively as you can, and avoid Career-Limiting Actions. Chapter 11 has more details. Firstly, though, we need to check whether you are clinging to the wreckage in survivor mode because of difficulties working out where your career is going.

Keeping alert to change

If you think your organization has shaken up everything possible, don't get too comfortable. The trend is that reorganization and structural change is following an increased pace. So how can you make sure that you avoid survivor mentality and begin to regain active control of your career?

One of the options is getting out of an organization, as we saw above. The biggest danger is that you repeat problems in your next job. Chapter 10 looks at ways of planning your next job move more carefully.

To build on where you are now, and to be effective within your organization, you need to be aware of internal and external factors, as demonstrated by Table 7.1.

Table 7.1   Looking inwards and outwards

External	Internal
What is your market doing?	What is your company's main focus?
Who is out there who can provide a better external service than internal suppliers?	What kind of results are seen as most urgent and appropriate?
What are your main competitors doing next?	What is your organization's next big issue?
How is your business going to change in the future?	How will organizational politics get in the way?

FIVE STEPS BEYOND SURVIVAL MODE

To move on from survivor mode to a position where you are beginning to thrive, you need to:

1. Get a new perspective on your job

2. Understand why perceptions matter

3. Expand on your job description

4. Understand and handle organizational politics

5. Anticipate changes in your field of work.

1. Looking at your job from the outside in

A great interim step is to take what marketing specialist Philip Spencer calls an 'outside in' view of your company. Essentially, this is about looking at your job from the perspective of an outsider. Is your contribution to the company clear? Would an outside observer see and value your contribution? Secondly, how does the work you do relate to the kind of work done by other people in other organizations? How is that work valued (salary, status, resources, etc.)?

Look at the way your company brings in outside expertise, in terms of either consultants or other suppliers. If you can fill the gap, why are they ignoring you? It could be because no one has challenged the idea that the best talent lies outside the organization, or it could be that your 'offer' is seen as weak compared with that of outsiders.

2. Understanding why perceptions matter

Look at the people who fast-track their way up the ladder in organizations. Are they always the most skilled? The most meticulous when it comes to looking after customers? The best at achieving targets? Sometimes, but more often it is not the true performers on an objective scale, but the people who *appear* to be doing the right things.

The cynics usually mumble at this point about toadying your way up the slippery pole, about spin-doctors and self-publicists. Well, a great deal of that goes on, too, but few long-term careers are built on such shaky foundations, largely because people need very good memories to remember the lies they told last week, and you can't fool all the people all of the time.

In reality, being 'in the right place at the right time' is about *perception*, which can be a matter of accident, but is far more commonly a matter of conscious or unconscious design, as Table 7.2 makes clear.

Table 7.2 How do you position yourself?

Unconscious positioning	Conscious positioning
Your boss happens to notice that you handle a difficult customer well	You share with your boss what you learned about handling a difficult customer, and ask her advice about doing it even better next time.
You cover someone else's work	You use the chance of covering for someone else's work to meet new people and ask questions about how another area of work is done.
You learn new skills in your own time	You seek to apply new skills by seeking opportunities to try out new activities at work which will benefit you employer.
You do something beyond the call of duty	You record and pass on customer feedback. You also pass on the successful techniques that achieved you the good feedback.
You dislike public praise	You seek one-to-one feedback on how you can improve, and seek opportunities to share your techniques with others.
You perform tasks to an excellent standard, and you're aware of the short cuts to success	You share your expertise with others by passing on tips and insights. You are given the chance to train or coach others.

3. Pushing the boundaries of your job

How elastic is your job? How far are you boxed in by your job description? If you think your job can't be altered or expanded, is this a restriction in the job, the organization or your mind-set?

Take a good look at your job. How could you add maximum value to your organization by making the smallest changes to your job? How can you add more interesting (and more productive) tasks?

Think of your job description as a starting point rather than a destination. Many people in our survey identified as a key factor for success the willingness to take on responsibilities that are outside your job description, activities that position you with key decision makers.

Here's how Penny Beazley of Mossop Cornelissen & Associates in Toronto sees it: 'Broaden your horizons within the organization. Start networking formally or informally (offer to be part of a project or task team, lunch with them, etc.) with people in other departments (particularly those of influence and key customers and suppliers if possible. Find out how the position that you are aiming for links with these internal and external stakeholders and how that may change. Try to identify what is key to developing and sustaining a good relationship with these stakeholders, by finding out what is important for THEM to succeed and how you can support their success.'

4. Avoiding the minefields: handling organizational politics

What do we mean by organizational politics? Let's look at some of the descriptions used by perpetrators and victims. To those who enjoy politics, it's about competition, getting ahead, winning. To those who lose out because of internal politics, it's about deception, manoeuvring and an unhealthy interest in making sure others don't succeed. Politics at work often causes confusion, a lack of shared objectives and a failure to encourage talented workers. Ultimately it results in cynicism.

Let's take an example from an organization that must remain anonymous.

Jill works for an organization where nothing can change unless a decision is made by one of the divisional heads. However, to gain access to the head of division, you need to negotiate through their PAs. Two of these PAs are at loggerheads. If you go to Manager A, Manager B's PA will cut you out of the loop. A huge amount of energy in the company goes into playing off one PA against another. A critical decision behind any action is which lobby you support, and which you choose to have as an enemy.

Sound familiar? It's too common a model. Senior managers scoring points off each other is one thing, but it can easily become a question of friend or foe. Great ideas get shot down simply because they are supported by the wrong faction. However, politics within organizations is a fact of life, and something we have to learn to deal with, without losing our integrity, and also without losing our fair chance at opportunities to achieve promotion.

How do you deal with the politics?

You may believe that the simplest strategy is to side with the strongest party. Doing that, however, means that you play by house rules. It won't be long before you find yourself concealing information or telling half-truths. How long before you begin to relish others' misfortune? The first problem of playing organizational politics is that you only win by losing; by losing integrity, losing friends and losing a belief in yourself. Very few people go into retirement wishing they had been more cunning at work. Some of them wish that they had more real friends.

Very few people enjoy organizational politics, so why do we put up with them? Partly because wherever you find people, you find some degree of political manipulation. Sometimes we're unaware of what's really going on: look back at all the times when you have been complicit, perhaps in an unwitting way, perhaps because of good motives. When has your behaviour been manipulated? How did it make you feel? If people around you say that's how you need to behave in order to get on, perhaps it's time to challenge that idea.

But how do you survive in a politicized environment, when you're supposed to take sides, toe the party line, say which side you're on? Table 7.3 offers a 20-point checklist for dealing with the politics inside an organization.

Table 7.3 Dealing with the politics

1. Be aware of the politics	That's more than being aware of your discomfort: you need to recognize the people who are the key influencers in the organization.
2. Look at the damage	It's often healthy and useful around you to help identify what goes wrong as a result of playing politics: the deals that are missed, the talent that leaves the organization. Discuss the downside with your colleagues.
3. Watch your back	Are you treading, inadvertently, on someone else's toes? Are you in somebody's way? Many honest, diligent people just don't see the knife coming in their back. Recruit or work alongside others who have better 'radar' than you.
4. Draw your line in the sand	Before the crunch comes, be clear about what you are not prepared to do to win.

5. Be honest	There really is no other policy, and you have to have a tremendous memory to tell lies in an organization. But remember that being honest doesn't give you carte blanche to criticize others. See number 6.
6. Praise or be silent	Remember your mother's advice: 'if you can't say anything nice, don't say anything at all'. Try to find something positive to say about your colleagues, or keep your peace.
7. Avoid gossip	OK, it's fun, but be careful to spot the line between discreet observations and character assassination. Distance yourself from 'toxic' attitudes and people.
8. Find allies and avoid enemies	It helps to have people on your side, but recruit them by helping them, providing useful information and showing you do a great job.
9. Identify the politics-free zones	There are usually some key managers or decision makers in organizations who manage to bypass the cutting and thrusting. Get them on your side, and follow their strategies.
10. Check how far your success means someone else's failure	Getting promoted requires competition, but doesn't have to cause someone else's downfall.
11 Accentuate the positive	You may find yourself surrounded by negative comments and thinking. It sometimes takes only a small effort to encourage people to see the glass as half full rather than half empty.

Continued

12. Move out of cynical teams	Cynical teams achieve very little, because they start from the position that it's all been tried before and there's no point anyway. If you're in a team like this and step 9 fails, try independent activity.
13 Seek win/win	Even in a highly politicized environment, it's possible to offer solutions that are a genuine win for both parties.
14. Be consistent	It's no use having integrity one day and being a conniving manipulator the next.
15. Do what you say you will do	Try it; it gets results. Fail to deliver (without explanation) and everything you say becomes an empty promise.
16. Set 10% of your time aside to help others	Consider this time well invested, and do it because you can, not because of any leverage it gives you.
17. Help your boss to win gracefully	Make your boss look good, but not at the expense of making someone else look bad.
18. Keep integrity as your surprise card	You know what 'integrity' means to you. Stick to your principles and don't dilute them. You may be the only person being straight and honest in your organization; if that's true, you are its greatest asset! Often the honest, non-manipulative strategy is the one that surprises.

19. Lose gracefully	If others jump the queue, push you aside or outmanoeuvre you, don't be tempted to play by the same rules. He who lives by the sword … .
20. Consider moving on	Don't use your failure to handle the politics as a stick to beat yourself. Organizational politics are hard to manage, even for the best operators. If you can't find a way to handle it, can't find the right allies, and your personal integrity is threatened too often, it may be time to move out. And when you do, don't let your message to your next employer be about the damage the organization has done to you.

When someone is really making your life difficult at work

What happens if someone is making your life miserable? Or if you are the person who has to fail in order for someone else to shine? These situations can be some of the most difficult to deal with in the workplace.

Remember that as an employee you have the legal right to enjoy a workplace that is free from bullying or victimization. If you are on the receiving end of this kind of behaviour, take advice. It may not always be effective to move immediately into a formal complaint: test the water first by discussing the problem with key influencers and decision makers. An informal reprimand or a quiet word is often less of a problem than beginning formal proceedings. It's worth thinking about the *outcome* that you have in mind: do you want retribution, or simply the opportunity to get on with your job? Sometimes it's better for your health to walk away from these battles.

Many situations are irritatingly intangible: life is being made uncomfortable for you, but there is no solid evidence; perhaps you're being set up to ensure that you fail, or given what the British Army calls 'all assistance short of actual help'.

The first step is to tell the difference between things you can do something about and things that are outside your control. Table 7.4 offers some ground rules, but refer back to Chapter 6 for more on aggressive self-promoters.

Table 7.4 Dealing with manipulative behaviours in the workplace

■ Often manipulative behaviour is prompted by fear. Look at what you might be doing that is threatening someone else's position. Make it as clear as you can that you are not a threat.

■ If you have to deal with difficult behaviours, focus on the behaviour, not the person. Saying 'I felt uncomfortable when you criticized my idea' is far less challenging than 'you're a negative person'.

■ Co-operate rather than compete, even if the ground rules suggest that competition is the only option. Sometimes workplace values can be shifted by not conforming to the dominant negative feeling.

■ Make sure that you are helpful to all your colleagues, not just the ones who can help you to get somewhere.

■ Avoid making critical remarks about colleagues, even if they seem out to get you. You never know how your words will be passed on. Saying nothing is a far easier position to defend.

■ If you have something better to offer than your colleagues, put the focus on your offer rather than on ways of making yourself look better than others.

■ Don't take it personally. You're not the first or the last person to be treated this way.

■ Don't seek revenge. If you do, you've just been manipulated into playing by a whole new set of rules.

5. Keeping alert to changes in the world of work

Career awareness, as defined in Chapter 3, requires a mix of information: about you, about the employers you would like to work with, and about the changing world of work.

Having looked at the main internal constraints to progress, it's equally powerful to look outside the organization. Chapter 5 helped you to gain a great awareness of the relative strengths and weaknesses of your company, but the difference between survival and growth may depend on your ability to understand the fast-changing nature of the wider marketplace.

We all know how dangerous it is to try to predict the future workplace, but it's important to try. How well can you predict what your job will be like in 5 years' time? The burst of the dot-com bubble meant that the markets suddenly lost faith in technology, but it hasn't gone away: every year computers get cheaper and more powerful. There are devices already in production that seem pure science fiction. Some may fail to catch on, others could completely revolutionize the way we work. Let's look at two simple examples.

Travellers in the underground railways of Tokyo find the carriages so crowded that it's impossible to read a newspaper. Now they can buy a pair of spectacles where one lens is converted to a mini-projector capable of displaying web pages. We are close to the point where we will be able to wear computer terminals as glasses or watches. How far away is the intelligent contact lens? And if you can access several million databases by blinking, what does that do to any job that involves communication or research?

The second major area of development is that those of us lucky enough to be born in the Western world are living longer, and we are healthier in our old age. Our children have a significant chance of living beyond the age of 100. The workforce, and consumers, are ageing.

The combination of changing work patterns and cheap technology has brought about a number of important trends (Table 7.5). How many of them are relevant to your job? What trends should you actively monitor? What are the trends that will give you an advantage?

Figure 7.5   Work trends

Where work is done	Data processing, banking services and call centres have all recently been transposed to low-cost environments. There has been a huge increase, for example, in call centres in India. Entire manufacturing plants have been transposed from the USA and UK to China and other developing countries. As technology becomes cheaper, many more service industries will follow.
How work is done	The UK has predicted a huge increase in homeworking for some years. This hasn't yet had the predicted impact, possibly because of the social benefits of actually attending a workplace. This may change quickly, particularly if road congestion increases or fuel costs rocket.
Who does the work?	As the workforce ages and travel problems continue (e.g. gridlocked motorways and air travel delayed by long security processes), time becomes the most important commodity. We already seek to find ways of delegating our home tasks (ironing, walking the dog, childminding, etc.), and it's likely that we will follow the same strategy with work activities (avoid those dreary book-keeping tasks by delegating them online to someone on the other side of the world?)
How will people be employed?	The past two decades have already seen a real flexing of categories: employed,

fixed-term contracts, subcontractors, temps, interim managers, consultants, associates, etc. It seems likely that we will see far more of this fragmentation, far more 'portfolio' careers, and more occasions where we negotiate the parameters of our relationship with an employer.

What experience will be considered valuable?	21st century employers have already redefined the ideal skills profile several times. As technical skills are automated, interpersonal skills become ever more important. Organizations change so rapidly that they need people with excellent change and project management skills.
What roles are most likely to change?	Essentially, any functional jobs that can be done online (producing communications, processing accounts, handling distribution, etc.) will move into low-cost regions. As a result, the jobs that remain in the developed world will either be 'high touch' (with highly developed interpersonal skills), immediate (you can't get your dustbin emptied online) or complex (calling on know-how, specialist knowledge and face-to-face consultation). As we value our leisure time increasingly, it seems likely that the 'high-touch' area will continue to include a wide range of personal services, from shopping assistants to cocktail mixers.
The demise of traditional career routes	Predictions suggest that most of us will experience not just regular job change, but possibly three or four changes of occupational field during a working lifetime. The skills and mindset you begin your career with won't be the set you finish with.

INTEGRATING LIFE AND WORK

Working to goals that are bigger than work

It seems increasingly common to find clients who are seeking promotion and a more stimulating job, but are also confused about what they want to get out of work and life. In its strongest manifestation this may be some kind of career crisis; for most it's a sense of unease. This can be precipitated by redundancy, by a personality clash at work, or by rejection from the job market. Their questions are about what they have to offer and what the market is like, but the underlying puzzle seems to be 'What is my work really for?' Sometimes it's necessary to take a slight detour on the way from survival to achievement, by taking this question seriously.

The meaning of work seems to become increasingly important to us as we get older. It relates closely to what Carl Jung called *individuation*. Individuation is a complex process that affects us differently, but it's essentially a time when we review what life is about. This new perspective on life can sometimes be described as a midlife crisis, or for others it comes across as a calm maturity. It's a time when we can become more comfortable with who we are and less concerned about impressing others. It's common for time itself to be the main reason (a sense of mortality), but a range of life events can prompt these feelings, including divorce, redundancy or health problems. Another common prompt is a bereavement, particularly the loss of one or both parents.

What is true for most people experiencing individuation is that we look at our past and try to make sense of it, and we feel the need to make important decisions about how we spend the rest of our working life. In the words of the great 1950s' song, we wake up one morning and say *'Is that all there is'*?

The idea of individuation springs from the work of Carl Jung, who argued that many people undergo a major transition or midlife crisis between our late 30s and mid-50s. Our earlier life, he believed, is a time when we are preoccupied with establishing ourselves in the world, and with the desire to fulfil the goals that stem from our biological urges. In later life we begin to see the finiteness of our existence and become more concerned with realizing our core personal, spiritual and even religious values. We individuate or find our way through the mass of competing motivations and desires to a more whole sense of purpose and self, and in recognising our true values we may well leave behind some the of the purposes, goals and activities of an earlier time, because they no longer satisfy us or even seem meaningful. This can obviously impact upon our feelings regarding the career we have chosen. It may mean we become disenchanted or burned out, or we may seek to find some new way of expressing our core values in a way that displaces our career path.

If this process is resolved successfully, the individuated self will tend to regain the capacity to see life positively. Where individuation is unsuccessful, it may cause continued unhappiness and a sense of being at odds with life. In the longer term, the individuated self is able to approach old age, and ultimately death, with an increasing sense of psychological wholeness or completeness.

Stuart Robertson, Occupational Psychologist

Aligning work and life goals

A final consideration in looking at external and internal factors, and one that will enable you to thrive in the long run, is to find a useful way of thinking about your life/work balance.

Much has been written on this subject in recent years. Very often we are made to feel that there is an ideal life/work balance. There isn't – it's all about what works for you. It's not a question of beating yourself up for the things you don't or can't do, but working actively to improve the margins of your life where you have some influence.

Many people talk about the things they would like to do with their life, but they are rarely asked how they would like to quantify these activities. Try it this way. If you think that you would like to do something for, say, at least one day a month, then you might try to block out one day in your diary and ring-fence it. Alternatively, you might work out what that would mean in terms of time in a typical week. One 8-hour day a month translates into roughly 2 hours a week, or about 25 minutes a day during the working week. Even assuming that you are only 50 per cent successful, very few of us can really fail to find 12 minutes a day to do something we've been promising to ourselves for years. Perhaps you want to improve your conversational Italian? Twelve minutes a day, every day, will dramatically increase your vocabulary.

You may feel that your goals can't be achieved in small bursts of activity. For example, it's difficult to pick up a complex skill in such short bursts. And what if your priority activity is, for example, taking longer holidays with your partner? However, these 12 minutes a day can also be used for planning or just even *thinking,* to enable you to create the time that matters. The important thing is that you distinguish between the ideal and the real: not just what you'd like to do, but what you *will* do. This is a principle that applies not only to work objectives but also to life goals: how much longer are you going to put off the things that really matter to you? And how can you integrate these goals into having a successful career? The answers are sometimes complicated and often unacceptable, but require a strong focus on the overall balance of your life.

EXERCISE 7.1 – LIFE PRIORITIES

One of the misunderstandings about work/life balance is that there is a preferred or an ideal balance. This can easily become one more reason to beat yourself up: *my life balance is wrong*. What matters is deciding what balance you think is important to you (and to your growth and well-being) and your family, and then taking an objective look at where your time is actually spent.

Joëlle Warren reinforces comments made by many in our survey about the right work/life balance: 'Don't win in business and lose in life – your family and friends deserve more than what's left after you've give your best to your work and they'll still be there when the job's gone.'

The writer Matthew Fox writes perceptively of the way that work can become addictive:

Behind some parental compulsion to bring home exaggerated amounts of pay is often a flight from the joy of living life here and now in the family – as if the future were more important than the present. ... We ought not to postpone living because of work or because of our plans for buying something with the money we make.

(*From* The Reinvention of Work, *Harper Collins, 1994*)

Reflecting on your life balance isn't about juggling your diary, but thinking about what work adds to life, and detracts from it. Complete Table 7.6 below to work out what activities outside paid employment are important to you, thinking about both time for yourself and time for others.

Table 7.6 Life priorities

Read through the checklist of activities below and tick the appropriate box. Some may be things you do frequently, others may be things you do rarely. NOTE: Your time may be filled with activities which are 'important' to other people (e.g. caring for a sick relative). For this exercise, focus on the activities that are important and enjoyable for *you*.

If there are any activities you wish to add, include them at the bottom of the table.

	1 NOT important to me and NOT enjoyable	2 Important to me but NOT enjoyable	3 NOT important to me BUT enjoyable	4 Important to me AND enjoyable	5 Very important to me AND enjoyable/ valuable to my life
Working for yourself (paid or unpaid work you do for interest)					
Quiet time with friends and family					
Playing with children					
Socializing with friends					

Table 7.6 (Contd)

	1 NOT important to me and NOT enjoyable	2 Important to me but NOT enjoyable	3 NOT important to me BUT enjoyable	4 Important to me AND enjoyable	5 Very important to me AND enjoyable/ valuable to my life
Listening to or playing music, singing, dancing					
Painting, drawing, being artistic					
Writing for pleasure or reflection					
Theatre, or concerts					
Watching movies					
Relaxing on my own					
Reading for pleasure					
Gardening					

Table 7.6 (Contd)

	1 NOT important to me and NOT enjoyable	2 Important to me but NOT enjoyable	3 NOT important to me BUT enjoyable	4 Important to me AND enjoyable	5 Very important to me AND enjoyable/ valuable to my life
Home improvement or decorating					
Being trained or learning on the job					
Studying in my own time					
Going on courses					
Reflecting/thinking/ meditating					
Looking after others					
Food shopping, cleaning					
Preparing meals					
Keeping fit, enjoying sport					

Table 7.6   (Contd)

	1 NOT important to me and NOT enjoyable	2 Important to me but NOT enjoyable	3 NOT important to me BUT enjoyable	4 Important to me AND enjoyable	5 Very important to me AND enjoyable/ valuable to my life
Walking					
Having health treatments, promoting my well-being					
Shopping for fun					
Making things with my hands					
Pet care					
Voluntary work for the community					
Worship, religious activity					
Other ...					

EXERCISE 7.2 – LIFE BALANCE

To complete this second half of the life balance exercise you need to work out roughly how much time you spend on each activity **per week**. If it is an occasional activity, make a rough estimate of how many hours you spend on it in a month, and then divide by 4.

1. Look at the choices you have put in column 5 of Table 7.5.

2. Choose the eight activities that matter to you most, and write them out in the eight boxes in Figure 7.1.

3. Now work out how much time you actually spend on each activity, shading in the appropriate number of rings out from the centre, using the **time key** opposite as your guide. For example, you might label one box 'Voluntary work' if this is a preferred activity. If you commit about 2 hours a week to this, shade in the segments as far as ring 3.

4. When you have finished, look at the overall circle. Where are the blanks?

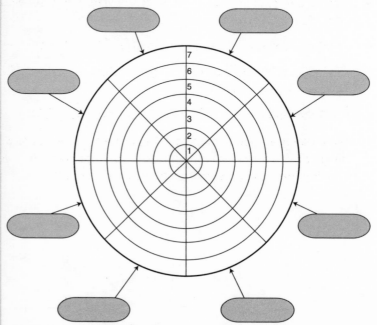

Figure 7.1   Life balance chart

Time key

1 Rarely: 15 minutes per week or less, possibly almost never

2 Occasionally: 30 minutes per week, possibly

3 Fairly regularly: maybe 1 hour a week or so

4 Regularly: 2 hours a week or so

5 Frequently: maybe 5 hours a week

6 Most days: 10 hours a week or more

7 Most of the time: 35 hours a week or more

'MUST DO' LIST

☑ What are you actively doing to make sure you are not seen as a target for redundancy?

☑ What are you doing to move from survive to thrive mode?

☑ How accurate is your perception of the way others see you in your company?

☑ What can you do to look at your job from the outside in?

☑ Are the politics in your organization getting in the way? If so, what can you do about it?

☑ What can you do to push the boundaries in your job?

☑ What changes would you like to make in your overall life/work balance? How will you integrate these changes into your working life and still position yourself well for promotion?

Cutting a Great Deal

This chapter helps you to:

▮ Overcome internal barriers to asking for a pay increase

▮ Work out a 'deal', even with voluntary work

▮ Understand how to work out what you're worth

▮ Negotiate a pay rise

▮ Plan for alternative outcomes

That which we obtain too easily, we esteem too lightly. It is dearness only which gives everything its value. Heaven knows how to put a proper price on its goods.

Thomas Paine

BARRIERS TO BEING PAID WHAT YOU DESERVE

Once you've discovered what a valuable asset you are to your organization, and you've moved on from survival mode to a real understanding of how you match your employer's preferred outcomes, you will quickly reach the point where you feel a need to negotiate a promotion or a pay rise.

Be clear about what you intend to achieve: more pay, or a different job? In Chapter 9 we will look at strategies for securing a promotion. Here we deal with the basics for negotiating a higher salary.

When it comes to pay negotiations, most of us wish we didn't have to be in the room. We see it as a nasty, grubby business, or a situation where all of the power is in someone else's hands. This means, sadly, that we fail to do for ourselves what the organization requires us to do every day: negotiate a fair deal. The difficulty is not negotiation as a skill in itself, but the fact that you are negotiating about *you*. Even seasoned sales or purchasing people find it hard to present a case for themselves.

What goes wrong? It seems to me that we are bad at doing two things: accepting praise and seeking reward. They are closely linked. If employment is about a psychological contract between employer and employee, the reason you are in work is essentially to fulfil a deal. You provide your energy, your expertise and your time, and the employer receives a tangible contribution to Key Result Areas (KRAs) (see Chapter 5).

What kind of rewards do you seek?

Is money the only way in which you are rewarded? It's probably better to start with the word *recognition*. How do you prefer to be recognized for your work? Go back to the list of motivators and career drivers that you came up with in Chapter 4.

The power (and weakness) of money

As we saw in Chapter 4, money is the easiest motivator to talk about and is often seen as the primary career driver, but often has the weakest long-term effect. That doesn't, of course, mean that you shouldn't be paid what you deserve. In fact, working at a lower pay level than you are worth may be a cause for demotivation.

Many of us struggle with the idea of money. If you feel underpaid, the next section is for you. But remember that feeling underpaid isn't a matter of greed. There are plenty of reasons why you may want to negotiate a rise:

▌ You are working above your level of responsibility, and have done so for some time unrewarded.

▌ Your ideas and your contribution are not valued because of your pay grade.

▌ Others do the same job as you and are paid more, even though their results are no better than yours (or possibly poorer).

▌ You know what contribution you make to the bottom line of your organization, and you feel that you are not compensated accordingly.

▌ You know how much it would cost to replace you.

However, many people feel a great deal of discomfort talking about money at all. This can be for a variety of reasons, as outlined in Table 8.1.

Table 8.1 Reasons for not talking about money, and their consequences

I don't want to be seen as grabbing	Are you expected to negotiate a fair deal on behalf of your employer? If you can't do this for yourself, what does it say about your skill set? It's only grabbing if you take more than you deserve. Negotiating a fair settlement is a different matter.
Talking about money is grubby	The feeling of grubbiness passes quickly. Actually, most employers expect you to discuss financial matters openly and objectively.
I'm happy with the going rate	Fine, but do you know what the going rate is? Or are you merely accepting your employer's guesswork?
I don't have the confidence to fight my corner	This is a major block for a lot of people. Some tips: imagine you are doing it for somebody else. Research carefully, so you're presenting facts,

	not hunches. Offer opportunities rather than demands. Don't wind yourself up to the point where you will take questions or rejection personally. A well thought-out written proposal may be your answer.
I can live with what I earn	Fine, if it's true. However, if you feel you are underpaid compared with your colleagues or peers, this reduces your motivation and performance.
If I ask for a pay rise and don't get it, I'll feel forced to move on to a new job	Who invents these rules? This is negotiation by ultimatum: consent, or I go. Even if you win, holding a gun to your employer's head is disastrous for long-term relationships. Look for win/win, not killer moves.
Work is about more than money	True, at least in terms of the motivation of most people. But your salary is about more than your ego: it's what your labour buys in terms of time, leisure, accommodation, lifestyle or family commitments. You add value to your work so you can add value to other parts of your life. If you are a high earner, put money back into the economy by providing work for others, and step up your charitable contributions.
I am uncomfortable earning a high salary when other people work harder than me and earn less	Sadly, pay levels are not related to the quantity of work you do, and sometimes not always related to quality. There is a premium paid for scarcity and complexity, but there is usually some connection between what you are paid and the value you add, or save. This may be in straight pounds, or sometimes in profile – a hospital administrator may be paid

Continued

	more than a nurse because of avoiding PR nightmares rather than skill level.
Higher pay means bigger headaches	Possible, but not automatic. Look at the number of people who get promoted simply to keep them out of trouble!

If you feel underpaid, or seriously underpaid, this is a niggle that just won't go away. Chapter 4 should already have convinced you that feeling underpaid is a major demotivator. You're reminded of this every payday. Are you putting more energy into worrying about your pay level than you are into the job?

Voluntary work or low-paid projects

There are times in life when we offer our work for nothing. Society wouldn't function without the voluntary contributions of time and effort that go into parent–teacher associations, Scouts and Guides, Church groups, community projects, prison visitors, and so on.

The attractive thing about voluntary work is that it clearly makes a contribution to society or to your local community. It can also provide a great opportunity to build up your skills. Handled well, voluntary work contributes to your career. You may pick up transferable skills that lead to paid work, or you may discover learning opportunities.

Sometimes the line between paid and unpaid work can become blurred. Consider, for example, the following three examples of unpaid employment:

■ a volunteer company adviser whose advice is not taken as seriously as a less qualified but salaried manager

■ a charity administrator who is not given support or training

▌ a training consultant who is offering free sessions, but cannot get the client company managers to commit to a date.

The problem in many cases is, essentially, this: *people value what they pay for*.

It's a reasonably good strategy to offer unpaid or low-cost work when you are starting up your own business, or if you are seeking work experience to bolster your CV. When you do this, remember to look for a 'deal' nonetheless. You may, for example, offer to provide your expertise over a fixed period at no charge, but make sure that you ask in return for tangible commitment, for example:

▌ travelling and other expenses

▌ access to key people in the organization

▌ the opportunity to attend key meetings

▌ honest and accurate feedback at the end of the project

▌ a positive reference, again at the end of the project.

The last point is crucial. Having undertaken one project you can honestly talk to future organizations about 'what I normally do ... ', and you can point to at least one past success. If the position is entirely voluntary, the deal should include learning opportunities and resources, as well as real feedback.

Failing to convince your employer or client to give you anything back for your time will make it much more likely that your contribution will be taken far less seriously, and you may find your voluntary contribution rather unfulfilling.

Identifying your true pay range

In paid employment you'll find it helpful to work out what the right 'deal' is between you and your employer.

It is a reality that sometimes people find it hard to break through a particular pay barrier. The odd thing is that this is as much to do with psychology as economics. Put in the crudest form, the following statement seems to be true: if you feel you are worth £20,000 a year, you will earn £20,000 a year. This self-imposed picture will actively limit your options. The opposite – believing you are worth £100,000 and so automatically getting it – isn't so straightforward; you can't just pick a figure out the air. However, what you can do is to conduct a personal pay review:

▌ What is your job worth, on average, on the open market? What are the upper and lower points of the pay scale for your job?

▌ What salary would your employer have to pay to replace you?

▌ What factors prompt an employer to pay above-average rates of pay?

▌ What would you have to offer to secure a pay in the top 10 per cent pay band for your occupation and sector?

If your job is rarely advertised on the open market, how do you know what it's worth? It's surprising how many employers pick a figure out of the air when advertising a new position. The reality is that, in terms of responsibility, know-how and experience, there really is very little difference between a £30,000 job and a £40,000 job, and even less difference between a £50,000 job and a £75,000 job. It's a question of employer and market expectations, and a certain amount of guessing on behalf of recruiters.

Negotiating pay is like any form of negotiation; you need to begin from a position of knowledge. How do you find out the pay range for your occupation? Here are some suggestions:

▌ Advertised vacancies: scrutinize the stated requirements.

▌ Search online job boards by sector and region.

▌ Keep active links with professional institutes or other bodies where fellow professionals gather.

▮ Refer to data published by the salary surveys (e.g. IDS or The Reward Group), surveys published by trade magazines, or free online data published by the Office for National Statistics.

▮ Network with recruitment consultants: they can often give you good feedback on market factors and pay rates.

If you ever want to find out what a job pays, you will rarely be successful if you ask directly. Better, for example, to get a broad feeling for the market rate, add 10 per cent, and then approach a recruitment consultant or employer and say 'I understand that a job at this level pays around £xxx – is that about right?' Whether you get confirming noises or a sharp intake of breath will tell you a great deal.

When job seeking you should only negotiate pay when the employer has decided they can't live without you. Similarly, the best time to renegotiate your salary is when your employer is most aware of your 'offer', most aware of the value you bring to an organization.

20 STEPS TO GETTING A PAY RISE

A word of warning: don't try all of these techniques at once. Choose your time carefully and work out an approach that will be appropriate.

If your boss is the right person, plan the discussion very carefully. Don't try to negotiate on a day when he's been carpeted for weak cost control! A good time is when you have just received praise for doing something well. A bad time is when your company is under financial strain or has just lost a key client. Don't let the fact that your company is laying off staff put you off asking for a pay rise (or a promotion, for that matter), very often companies take active steps to retain key staff at times like this.

When planning your approach, use the checklist below. Make notes carefully over a couple of weeks and research your background material carefully.

Step 1: Who decides?

First of all, identify the decision maker. Is it your boss or someone else? Who makes the final decision? Are there any external constraints such as company policy (e.g. pay rises are only given at certain times of year). If so, ask around to identify exceptions to the rule; you can usually find them.

If your boss is the decision maker, think carefully about the way that he or she likes to handle information, questions and new suggestions. Some managers are very happy to respond on the spot, whereas others need some thinking and reflection time. If you have a reflector, it might be a good idea to flag up what you want to talk about in advance, and possibly provide a written summary of the background evidence. It's not a good idea to state in advance exactly what kind of a figure you are looking for.

Be aware also that some managers become defensive. No matter how carefully you make your case, what they will hear is 'you're not treating me right' or 'I'm unhappy'. Be careful to reinforce your suggestions for change with plenty of positive comments.

Step 2: Do your research

Go back to the earlier part of this chapter to identify methods of working out what your job is worth. Don't go into a pay negotiation without:

- an upper figure or range: your target zone. DON'T guess on what the job is worth. Find out the upper and lower points of the salary typically paid for this kind of job. Rehearse all the reasons why you should be paid in the top 25 per cent of this band

- a fallback position: what you are prepared to accept

- an alternative fallback position: what you are prepared to offer and accept if no additional money is available. (This is a good time to negotiate conditions that match your main career drivers; see

Chapter 4.) The advantage of negotiating non-financial factors at this point is that your boss may be relieved to be able to offer you something low on cost and high on imagination.

Step 3: Clarify your objectives

Whether you're springing a meeting on your boss at an opportune moment or conducting a prearranged meeting, make it very clear what the meeting is about. Try not to be vague by talking about 'prospects' or the 'future'. Make it very clear that you want to talk about your contribution to the organization and that you're asking for a pay rise.

Step 4: Don't get a pay rise and promotion confused

All too often a discussion about pay turns into a conversation about promotion, and vice versa. DO be very clear about the topic of your conversation. A promotion is unlikely to be something that you can negotiate as a result of a one-off meeting (although asking for a promotion can be a critical step). The danger is that your objectives become confused: you may end up with a new job title and little else. If you have set out to gain a pay rise, stick to that agenda. If your employer wants to talk about promotion, make that the agenda for a separate meeting.

Step 5: Create the right impression

DO look, act and sound like a person already holding down a job paying the kind of salary you want. Don't negotiate a pay rise in an old suit.

Step 6: Begin and end with positives

Because it's vital that you don't turn a pay negotiation into a complaints session, it's really important that you begin and end your 'pitch' (see below) on a positive note. Start with a statement like 'First of all I'd like to say how much I've enjoyed the job over the last 12 months'. Don't make it sound as if there is a huge 'but' coming along. Be clear: 'I'd like to think I have an exciting future here, and that I've got a lot to offer. And that's why I'm asking for a pay rise.' If the meeting ends up without that result, make sure you end positively but with a clear agreement about when the issue is going to be discussed.

Step 7: Make your pitch

Your opening needs to be about your contribution, and not about money. DON'T make your bid sound like a complaint. Be careful to ensure that you communicate how much you enjoy the job, particularly those parts where you have extended your job content.

Try something like 'I'm aware how much my job has grown, and how much more I'm contributing to the organization. I'd like you to review a number of things about my role, and the first thing is: I'd like to ask for a pay rise.'

Step 8: Watch for the brush-off

DON'T allow your approach to be brushed aside with a throwaway line; for instance, when you say 'I'd like a pay rise' your boss might answer 'Who wouldn't?'. It's a commonly used technique. Press on. If you think your boss will react that way, maybe it would be a good idea to set up a meeting with a clear agenda.

Step 9: Make your case, and provide evidence

Remember, the more your 'pitch' sounds like 'I want more money' the less welcome it will be. Your case should be about job content, responsibility and the *future* – how you will continue to contribute. Your boss may not be aware of how your job has changed and may not be aware of all the projects you are now running. Provide a list of your key responsibilities (before the meeting if this is useful).

Step 10: Focus on Key Result Areas

DO focus on what you are bringing to the deal, remembering to explain in 'win' language which means something to your employer. This is where you can draw upon the evidence you have discovered about the KRAs of your job and organization (see Chapter 5).

The points that you will emphasize will be:

I tasks you have accomplished that are 'above your pay grade'

I projects you have handled personally

I times when you have rescued victory from the jaws of defeat

I all the times you match KRAs in the job

I the many occasions when you have gone the extra mile.

Chapter 10 will give you some more tips on spotting your achievements. DON'T focus just on the past – describe what you can do in the future.

Step 11: Treat the conversation as normal

DON'T sound as if you are asking for something unusual or exceptional. The more your tone of voice suggests that this is a perfectly natural next step for the organization, the more it's likely to happen.

Step 12: Negotiate on your terms

DON'T be tempted to talk about what you 'need' financially. Talk about the value you add.

Step 13: Let your boss shoot first

DON'T jump in with a figure. Spell out your 'offer' first, and find out what your employer is prepared to put on the table. Even if your employer asks 'What did you have in mind?' it's worth at least one attempt to find out what might be possible: 'Perhaps you could let me know what kind of pay range might be available?', and when you have an answer ask: 'What would I need to do to be paid in the top end of that range?'

Step 14: Don't accept the first offer as final

If your pitch is good, there's no reason why you shouldn't achieve a pay rise. Thousands do every week. DON'T believe that the first offer, particularly if it's made quickly, is the last word. This is where your background planning is vital. How does the offered pay rise relate to your anticipated range? If you have to come back, reinforce your 'pitch' again and give clear, concrete reasons why the pay offer may not be enough.

Step 15: Seek 'and also' solutions

It may be that you have to accept a deal cut in a way you didn't expect. Your employer may, for example, ask you to take on additional responsibilities to prove yourself. You may get offered something much lower than your ideal salary. Remember that once the money issues are resolved, there are still other elements in the deal. You may be able to ask for an early review date. You may be able to negotiate a bonus or a better commission structure. You may be able to fix some demotivators – for example, trading in a company car that you find tax inefficient and moving to a car allowance scheme (or vice versa). DON'T forget that giving in on the money front gives you even more reason to seek solutions that relate to your non-financial motivators.

Step 16: Don't be coercive

DON'T hold a gun to your employer's head, such as 'I am getting offers from ... ' or 'I'll be forced to look for a job'. DON'T use an external job offer to force your employer's hand. Do that and you have no offer, just a threat. There's plenty of evidence around that this strategy is perceived as very threatening by employers, and the end result is often that the employee leaves the organization anyway, often for the wrong reasons. You might, just, get away with saying 'I'm being pestered by headhunters who keep offering me jobs, which has prompted me to think carefully about why I enjoy this role. However, I'd like to have a meeting to look at my pay package.'

Remember, it's a negotiation, not a stand-off.

Step 17: Be prepared for a deferred decision

DON'T be surprised by a blocking response ('my hands are tied ... ') or a delaying response ('I'll have to run this by the MD ... '). The result of both approaches is usually that the issue is transferred to someone else. The problem is that the only message that becomes transferred is that 'Joe wants a pay rise', which if you're not present can easily translate into 'Joe's complaining'. Offer to contribute to further discussions in person or in writing so that your message can't be misinterpreted.

Step 18: Negotiate, negotiate

DO negotiate like a pro. Here are a few tried and tested techniques.

▌ Work out the difference between what you are asking for and what the employer is offering. Let's say you are after a £2000 a year pay rise, and your employer offers £1000. Divide it by 50, then say 'We're talking about a difference of £20 a week. We pay more than that in photocopying/coffee/stamps ... '. (Remember that every £1000 per year is roughly £20 a week.)

▌ Relate your proposed pay increase in monthly terms to the annual bottom-line contribution of the job, e.g. 'For £2000 a month salary costs you're going to achieve at least £90,000 savings (or sales, or profit, or output) next year'.

▌ Reinforce the idea that your memory and knowledge are huge assets.

▌ Invite (but very subtly) your employer to think about the opportunity costs of not having you around. You might be saying something like 'We're both aware of the time and trouble it would take to go to the open market to fill this post'.

Step 19: Bang the table, but gently

DO stand up for yourself, but be assertive rather than aggressive. Remember that you are now exercising a toughness that your employer probably expects you to demonstrate to others, particularly suppliers. You're also using negotiation and problem-solving skills, so by demonstrating your ability to cut a deal you are, in effect, adding to the evidence about why you should be paid more.

Step 20: Think about alternative outcomes

If the employer won't move on the money, ask for an early salary review date or an enhanced bonus, or some other way of improving the package quickly. DON'T give away concessions unnecessarily; for example, accepting a pay rise now but agreeing to skip a pay review next year. DO look at alternatives. If you can't get a pay rise, can you use your position of leverage to make the job more interesting?

'MUST DO' LIST

☑ Begin your research now into what your job is worth. Establish in your mind very clearly what your job is worth inside and outside your company.

☑ Set clear upper and lower parameters for what you are prepared to accept in terms of a pay rise.

☑ Plan your approach to your pay negotiation carefully, in terms of preparation, timing and style of approach.

☑ Keep your bid positive and focused on the future. Rehearse what you will say with a supportive friend.

☑ Plan your fallback positions in advance, including the possibility that nothing works!

Upward, Ever Upward?

This chapter helps you to:

▌ Plan before you pitch

▌ Spot career traps

▌ See how people get promoted beyond their competence and confidence

▌ Rethink appraisals, and gain more from them

▌ Negotiate a promotion

The difference between a successful career and a mediocre one sometimes consists of leaving about four or five things a day unsaid.

Anon

PLANNING CAREFULLY BEFORE PITCHING FOR A PROMOTION

Promotion or pay rise?

In Chapter 8 we looked at the tools you'll need to negotiate a pay rise. This chapter looks at an associated issue: how to work specifically towards a promotion and how to negotiate it when it becomes a possibility.

It's important to see the difference between negotiating a pay rise and seeking a promotion. One is about being paid more for the job you're doing. That may be exactly what you need at the moment in terms of your personal goals, but the nature of the job stays the same. Seeking a promotion should be about changing the overall balance of the work you do, and often about acquiring work that is more challenging – and more demanding, too.

Plan before you pitch

Many respondents to our survey in Chapter 2 reinforced the idea that promotions won't automatically chase you. If promotion does come along out of the blue, it's most probably because you are unconsciously demonstrating the right attitudes and behaviours. In a busy environment with an oversupply of data on a daily basis, managers miss key messages unless you make them clear. So, in short, you may well have to make a pitch and ask for a promotion.

To do so without preparation, however, is like trying to sell expensive products using the phone book: you have little idea of what people are looking for or how to sell it to them.

Planning a promotion is as complex and time-consuming as organizing any kind of project. It takes as much groundwork and thinking as making a job change, and sometimes more, as you are chasing a much narrower band of opportunity.

Your planning begins with the work we have covered in Chapter 5. How well do you know your organization? Next, moving on from your knowledge of Key Result Areas (KRAs), you need to work systematically through a one-person research project: what do I need to do to get promoted? Many of these issues are exactly the kinds of questions and evidence that you need to examine while preparing for an appraisal, as you will discover later in this chapter.

However, there are some particular areas of preparation to consider before actively seeking promotion, as Table 9.1 shows.

Table 9.1 Preparation before seeking promotion

Awareness	How well do I understand my organization? (See Chapter 5)
	What contribution am I really making to the big picture?
	What events or outcomes have I really influenced?
	Who depends on me and what I do?
	How do I perceive my strengths?
	What do my colleagues, my boss and key decision makers see as my strengths?
Job role	How clearly have I fulfilled my existing job role?
	What do I see as my biggest successes?
	What do key decision makers in the organization see as my biggest successes?
	What do I see as my failures?
	What do key decision makers in the organization see as my failures?
Others	Who performs a similar role to me at a higher or lower grade?
	Who else has been promoted recently? Why?
	Who has been promoted from my grade in the recent past? What did they do to achieve it?
Next steps	What changes to my job would be most acceptable/exciting to me?
	What changes to my job would be most acceptable/exciting to the organization?
	What's the most obvious next step for me as my boss would see it?
	What other steps are possible?

You will see that many of the questions in Table 9.1 require you to do more than think: you'll need to ask other people questions. Finding out how others see you is vitally important. Sometimes you pick this up from passing comments, but it's helpful to know as much as you can. Trusted colleagues will give you a straight answer to the question 'What does X think of me?', but sometimes it's easier to ask about the task rather than about you: 'Why was that helpful? How could I have done a better job?'

'Broaden your horizons within the organization' is a theme of many responses to our survey in Chapter 2. This is about networking formally or informally. On the formal level you may offer to be part of a project or task team. Informally, you may find an opportunity to have lunch or coffee with members of other departments. You may also rub up against them working on charitable projects.

You may also find it useful to talk to people outside your organization: consultants, suppliers, linked organizations, sometimes even competitors.

The message is clearly this: when looking for promotion, keep your eyes and ears open, not only in work but outside work, because sometimes opportunities occur in surprising circumstances. You'll also find it helpful to manage relationships around you at work, particularly with your boss.

Communicate with your boss sparingly and effectively

'Learn to manage your boss' is one of the key messages from our research, particularly as your direct boss is the person who can either ensure your promotion or prevent it. Your path upwards within the organization depends on this relationship, so you need to use your contact time with your boss economically. Popping in for a 'quick word' too often makes you a distraction, and also reinforces the idea that you cannot work unsupervised.

Plan your meetings with your boss carefully. Have a written agenda if that's your boss's style, but in any event have a verbal agenda ('I'd like to talk to you about three things – have you got a couple of minutes?'). Stick to your agenda, and get out as quickly as you can (unless invited to do otherwise): it may be a day when your boss has an agenda, too.

Another key finding from those who have achieved promotion in the past is that you need to keep your boss informed, but not overinformed. A good idea is to produce a weekly report using the 20/5 principle. This is a document that takes you up to 20 minutes to write and your boss no more than 5 minutes to read. Under no circumstances should your main report exceed one page of A4 (occasionally you may have attachments such as copy letters). The workplace is awash with information, so keep your boss (and other decision makers) well informed, but be brief.

'Make sure your boss knows your achievements', says Julia Robertson, MD of Carlisle Staffing Services. 'Ask your boss "is there anything more I could be doing to do my job better, or to develop myself for the next step on the ladder?". Make your boss accountable for helping you achieve the job you want.'

Career coach Derek Osborn asserts that you can create opportunities for yourself through your manager: 'Volunteer for more responsibilities, write terms of reference for the kind of more responsible job or project that you would like and give it to the boss'.

Reading your boss's style

Things often go wrong in the workplace where you have two or more people who misread each other. This isn't about getting on with people so much as reading the way they like to be communicated to, the way they handle new ideas, the way they deal with criticism, and how much they care about things such as detail. Exercise 9.1 encourages you to check out your boss's style, and to see how aware you are of problems.

Exercise 9.1 – Working Out Your Boss's Thinking Style

In Table 9.2, tick the one style under each heading that you think best describes your line manager (don't leave this lying around at work!).

Table 9.2 Your boss's thinking style

My manager is most concerned with			
Results	People	Principles	Processes
My manager is most concerned with			
Fine Details	Explanations	Activity	The big picture
My manager's style with decision making is			
Democratic	Consultative	Delegating	Autocratic
My manager's style of working in a team is			
Chairperson	Ideas person	Facilitator	Encourager
My manager is most concerned with			
Facts	Image	His feelings	My feelings
In a meeting my manager prefers to be the			
Boss	Ideas person	Co-ordinator	Analyst
My manager values in other people			
Detail	Ideas	Teamwork	Innovation
My manager prefers feedback on his/her work			
In private	In a small team	In public	Never
My manager likes new information			
Informally, and on the spot	Informally, but with clear facts and explanations	Informally, but with plenty of notice	Formally in writing

Learn to manage your boss as this is the only person who can sack you or prevent you getting promoted. He/she is the most important person in your career especially at the beginning. Analyse and identify the characteristics of the managers promoted to senior positions in the company you work for. If the company promotes commodity traders to senior positions and you are a technical manager then the chances are that you will not be promoted, indeed the body of traders will ensure that you don't get promoted. Promotion is about being in the right place at the right time, about 40% of the time, knowing the right people (40%) and about ability (20%). Looking the part is also important as is the image you project. A smooth operator with limited brain power will do better than a super intelligent type who cannot express him/herself. Head Office is the place to be if you want to be promoted. It is also the place that your reputation can be destroyed even if you don't work there.

Fred Mahoney, former MD of the Dry Corn Ingredients Division of Cargill Plc, now Visiting Professor at the University of Liverpool Management School

CAREER TRAPS AND HOW TO AVOID THEM

It's useful to be aware from the experiences of others that there are many identifiable things that get in the way of career progression. There are a number of career traps: dead ends or blocks that take you one square forward on the chess board, but mean that you are unable to move any further.

Trap 1: Being flattered into accepting a promotion

On occasions we feel pressurized to apply for internal positions because others suggest that we would be 'great for the job'. We feel flattered, and we don't want to let down the person who suggests that we apply, particularly if it's somebody we respect.

You shouldn't take any job just because someone else tells you you'd be perfect for it, and you certainly shouldn't take a promotion on these grounds without checking the job out carefully. It's important not to put on rose-tinted spectacles when considering a job. The difficulty with an internal position is that *both* taking it without reflecting *and* turning a promotion down could be **Career-Limiting Actions** (see Chapter 11). Take care, then, to investigate a position quietly and make sure it is a good match for you, and a good stepping stone. If it's not, and you are still put under some pressure by a boss or mentor to apply, take time to negotiate carefully: don't be negative or give the impression you are turning down a gift, but state assertively what it is you are looking for, and you may even have a better chance of encouraging your employer to change the job or offer you another.

Trap 2: The wrong direction

Sometimes a career trap looks and feels more like a dead end. This can sometimes be because you've become over-specialized, but also because you may be in a part of the organization that has become disconnected from the main event. Here, a sideways move into a department or unit that is more centre stage may seem like a good idea.

Trap 3: Hitting the ceiling

The idea of a glass ceiling is familiar to most of us. It's an invisible barrier above which certain kinds of people cannot progress. The 'glass ceiling' model is often applied to women, and it is true that more than a quarter of a century after equal pay legislation was introduced in the UK, women are on the whole paid less than men and have more limited access to senior positions in the organization. However, the glass ceiling principle often seems to apply to other groups, such as non-graduates or those without particular kinds of experience.

Anyone looking to break through such a barrier needs to take notes from others who have done so before them. It's a hard enough job anyway, but trying to invent new strategies is harder still. Seek out people who have trodden this path before and find out how they did it. For those particularly interested in the problems experienced by women in career transition, I would recommend *Stepping Up – Women's Guide to Career Development* by Nadine Kazerounian (McGraw-Hill, 2001).

Where the glass ceiling is set around certain kinds of qualifications or experience, you essentially have the same problem as a career changer faced with a job that appears to have strict entry requirements. The advice to career changers is the same as the advice to those who seek promotion: seek out or encourage exceptions to the rule. Most organizational rules have clear exceptions. So find examples of people who have found a way around, through or over the obstacle facing you. If you turn out to be the pathfinder, you need to encourage your employers to rethink. Challenge the dominant mindset. If your employer sets a requirement that you cannot meet, ask why the restriction exists and show how you are a good match in other ways. If you're told that only graduates get to a certain pay grade, show how your training and the projects you have undertaken are equivalent to a degree. Few glass ceilings have a rational basis to them; it's mostly about continuing the status quo and 'the way we do things here'.

Trap 4: Becoming overspecialized

Specialist expertise is valued by organizations, but not necessarily in senior staff. It's a difficult balancing act. The job will often require you to acquire fairly specialized know-how and skills, but it's often best to adopt these on a project-by-project basis and move on each time to new challenges. It's an easier and apparently safer option to learn how to manage one kind of problem, and then repeat the experience. This isn't always the most powerful strategy for moving up within the organization. Specialist knowledge is the key if you intend to develop a portfolio or consultancy career. In a general management role it seems unwise to be overspecialized, although it's unclear whether this is because companies fail to promote those whose experience is too narrow, or simply because organizations don't believe that specialists look the part.

Many respondents to our survey suggested that moving from specialist to increasingly generalist roles was the key to promotion, for example Mike Wallwork: 'Providing you have strong communication and leadership skills a little knowledge of a lot of subjects goes farther than in-depth knowledge of a narrow business base in terms of career progression.'

In a number of industries there are many who have found that they get 'blocked' by being in a cul-de-sac, and this often happens to those in technical positions. At a very senior level, too, those with IT or accountancy specialisms sometimes find it hard to step into the very top jobs, unless they have, through choice or opportunity, acquired broader experience along the way. One of the key issues here is not just what's on your CV, but how you are perceived by the organization.

Trap 5: Getting into a rut

A career rut is a state of inertia. You recognize the symptoms when you are in one: you have probably stopped learning, your job offers few challenges, and your motivation to undertake tasks you have done before decreases every month. Why don't you get out of the rut? Because it's a *velvet rut*, and it's just a little too comfortable to get out of. The money's good, you have an easy journey to work, and the grass is always greener ...

Being in a rut can be a career trap because we start to lose awareness of our lack of energy and contribution. In a way, we become a little too relaxed about our performance. We start to take pride in the fact that we don't need to learn new-fangled ideas or techniques. We begin to lose touch with what's going on in our company and outside it in our industry.

There's only one way out of this trap. Adapt your rut into something different, or focus on the real reasons why you want to change.

Trap 6: Being pigeon-holed

The above section on becoming overspecialized demonstrates one kind of pigeon-holing. This can also happen when you're not a specialist. What happens is that your colleagues don't see you, but see a stereotype. This may, ironically, be because of one career-progressing action or idea. You succeeded in one area and succeeded in getting noticed, and that's the way you're seen for ever.

The only way out of this is to push out against the sides of your pigeon hole. Challenge people's assumptions by stating them: 'I expect you think I'm mainly interested in training. Actually, I've really enjoyed some of the client contact I've had recently … '

Be prepared for the fact that your communicated successes may, for a short while at least, create a fixed perception amongst colleagues and decision makers.

Trap 7: Accepting the poisoned chalice

Often the position we are flattered into accepting is the one where we are set up to fail from the outset. Many organizations have poisoned chalice jobs, for a range of reasons, which could include:

▌ A manager needs to be sacrificed on the altar of change. A change is necessary, but the person who institutes it is unlikely to survive in the job. Check this one out by finding out why change is necessary and who has a vested interest in opposing it.

▌ The role is never filled for more than 12 months at a time. This could be because of an overbearing boss.

▌ The job can't be done by one person who also needs to sleep and have any kind of relationships outside work.

Trap 8: Taking on a challenge without the resources to succeed

The last but biggest career trap is the mistake of taking on a role or task that has demanding targets or outcomes but does not have the matching level of resources to allow you to succeed.

This career trap is often the real deal-breaker, and the cause of many problems. It's what has been called the 'set-up-to-fail syndrome', where managers move into a vicious circle that ends up undermining underperformers. Authors Manzoni and Barsoux suggest that what happens is that managers start unconsciously to undermine the performance of the staff who report to them, through ineffective feedback and weak interventions, or sometimes by actively putting them in situations where failure is inevitable. The result is a downward cycle of negative perception:

The subordinate sees the boss as intransigent, interfering, and hypercritical; the boss sees the subordinate as inept, uncooperative, and indecisive. They are well and truly caught up in the set-up-to-fail syndrome.

The Set Up To Fail Syndrome,
(Harvard Business School Press, 2002)

A very simple example is where a manager constantly delegates to your weaknesses (so you continue to underperform) rather than to your strengths.

If you are given targets you cannot achieve with the resources that are made available, it's easy to get into a cycle which ends up with a reputation that you have been promoted beyond your competence. There is only one solution: to know before you take any job what problems need to be solved, to be aware of your strengths, and to encourage your employer to offer you projects that match your strengths. If you are offered a job that is effectively directed towards your weaknesses (e.g. it requires high attention to detail and you're a big picture person) then you are setting yourself up to fail.

Trap 9: Failing to manage others

There is some evidence from different management studies that you can fall into career trap by being seen as a poor manager of other staff. This, again, is a matter of perception rather than reality, and it can be a key factor when others come to discuss your potential for promotion. This is a tricky one in a number of ways because your superiors probably won't have first-hand experience of your style as a manager or supervisor. But they will judge you by the results of your team and by the number of problems that are generated along the way. A fairly clear sign of difficulties is where you experience above-average staff-retention problems, or your staff are regularly complaining about you to other managers.

You need to be aware of how far the performance of your team or your subordinates reflects on you, and also be aware that a good, productive relationship with those under your supervision may be taken as a benchmark characteristic for future promotion. Another way of expressing this is 'be careful how you treat people on your way up … '.

There are endless books written on this subject, but one principle stands out: whatever your management style, whether tyrant or guru, be consistent. Nothing disturbs staff like having to second guess which way up you're going to be in the morning.

RETHINKING APPRAISALS

We've moving towards the point of negotiating a promotion, looking at the preparatory ground you cover before your 'pitch'. You can achieve a great deal by thinking about the appraisal process.

You may be looking forward to your next appraisal meeting; others dislike the process and find it stressful or unproductive. Common reactions are that we don't know what's going to come up and we don't know what to say. Interestingly, many managers would also like to avoid appraisals. As a management tool, appraisal has many limitations. If it's used as a way of correcting behaviour or offering praise, it tends to be ineffective because of the long gap between meetings. Efficient managers know that most problems need fixing immediately, and the best way to offer praise is usually on the spot.

Appraisals can be negative. One manager said to me, 'I feel constrained by the system to say something negative – and it becomes an excuse for criticism on both sides.' If you find yourself dealing with negative feedback, try to concentrate on the observable behaviours that your boss wants to see, and the outcomes that need to be achieved. Don't let your personality get in the way, and don't blame others or 'the system' for your mistakes. South African HR specialist Andrew Bramley suggests that the real key is 'getting your ego out of the way when things don't go your way, solving problems without blaming everyone in your path'.

A good appraisal essentially asks the question 'How can we work better together?' It is your opportunity to turn things to your advantage. Linda Walmsley, Search & Selection specialist, says: 'If there is an appraisal scheme make the most of it. Get your manager to note your strengths and make sure that you take advantage of any development opportunities that are offered. This could be a specific training course or something as simple as being more self aware.'

Well-conducted appraisals are part of the retention process – your company asking "how can we build and retain our best people?" Experienced staff want new challenges but also want to remain loyal to their present employers.

Remember that the way that your manager *feels* at the end of the process is as important as the facts and details written down on the appraisal record. When you go into an appraisal you may like to use a checklist like the one given in Table 9.4.

Table 9.4 Your appraisal checklist

Reviewing your last appraisal

What actions were agreed at my last appraisal?

How far have I carried out the actions that were my responsibility?

What actions did my employer commit to?

Which of these actions have not been fulfilled? Which ones matter to me?

Role contribution

How have I developed my job since my last appraisal?

How have I moved outside my job description in predictable ways?

How have I moved outside my job description in *un*predictable ways?

What have been my successes?

How have I contributed to the organization's KRAs?

Where is the evidence?

Who has helped me? Who should I be praising?

What do I really enjoy about my job?

Future role development

What skills and know-how do I want to acquire in the future?

Which teams or individuals would I like to work with?

Which projects or clients would be perfect for me?

Which of my career drivers are not being fully addressed?

What will motivate me even more?

How might I be able to reduce or delegate tasks I find demotivating?

What should my employer be doing to retain me?

What specific projects or areas of responsibility can I suggest to improve my job?

What project ideas, initiatives or pilot studies can I suggest?

How can I communicate the benefits to my employer?

Who else do I need to convince?

What quick wins can I offer my employer that will benefit our customers and bottom line? (See also Chapter 11 on making your mark in a new job.)

The checklist in Table 9.3 begins with a quick check on what was agreed at your last appraisal. Think these points through carefully before you start. If you begin a meeting by apologizing for the things you committed to last year but have failed to deliver, the meeting is going downhill from the start.

Promotion decisions are often made on small pieces of evidence: a chance remark, a presentation you made at a meeting (covered in Chapter 6), a project you handled well, or a series of positive remarks and suggestions that you made during an appraisal. Imagine that a meeting to discuss your promotion prospects is being held 24 hours after this appraisal. What overall message would your boss be conveying?

The checklist also contains positive, concrete suggestions. A successful appraisal should include an win/win solution. What you are saying at your new-style appraisal is not 'I dislike ... ' but '*Here is an opportunity I have identified that draws on my top skills ... I will benefit from doing it because ... You will benefit if I do this because ... .*' Few employers can really deal effectively with 'I am unhappy with ... ', but equally there are few employers who do not respond warmly to 'Here's a great idea about how I can help you build business/do things more effectively/look after our customers': both parties will prosper and feel good about the deal. In this kind of language, it's much more difficult for an employer to say 'no'.

Don't expect to get everything covered in your first appraisal. Better to let your manager conduct the appraisal in his or her own style, and later in the meeting when you have a chance to bring up issues, introduce questions and statements that broaden the conversation. Ask for another opportunity (soon) to communicate your offer if it seems appropriate.

Try a pilot scheme

If your employer is unsure, make a conditional offer: people are more likely to accept a pilot scheme or a mini-project than a huge and permanent change. It's a lower risk option that is always more acceptable at every level in the organization because nothing is cast in stone. You're floating a practical experiment, and offering to come back with some results and feedback about how effective the pilot scheme was. Many fledgling projects become institutional norms without anyone blinking an eye. That's one of many ways in which new jobs are created.

Adding value and taking charge

Employers who come across the idea of the transformed appraisal sometimes feel challenged by the idea of workers taking charge of the process. But in an economy where staff are not just an asset but retain key knowledge, that's the reality of staff retention; we have more leverage, and more say in our futures. Employers often say *'but what if the employee wants something I can't offer?'* My reply is always: *'Then you've just received early warning of a retention problem.'* At least 50 per cent of the time it makes good economic sense to redesign the job of a key player rather than lose him or her to a competitor, an idea to keep up your sleeve when negotiating your future!

You should be encouraged to come to a meeting at least every 6 months with at least three suggestions of ways you could work more effectively and create new opportunities for the company. If your boss hasn't asked for this, then suggest it. If your boss is the kind of person who likes to be in control of information, it might be a good idea to mention it in advance of the meeting, possibly even in writing.

Don't forget that as your role develops you will be constantly redefining success and what motivates you (see Chapter 4). At first you'll enjoy the novelty of the role. Later you may get a buzz from completing projects or making things happen. Later there are other carrots, such as earnings potential or the possibility of learning.

Eventually in any job there comes a point when we need to identify opportunities to grow personally and professionally. Sometimes we outgrow jobs, sometimes we adapt them to suit our changing perspective.

So, when you are thinking up positive suggestions for your next appraisal, look at all the elements you can put into the mix. The answers may be partly financial (but don't waste an appraisal arguing about money; flag it up as an issue and secure a separate meeting). Just as often your solution will require an intelligent mix of new challenges new learning and a chance to grow.

NEGOTIATING A PROMOTION

Note that a great many of the techniques you used in Chapter 8 will also work in when you're negotiating a promotion, particularly in relation to working out a win/win offer to your employer. Here are some of the additional issues.

Is there a position available?

Identify the person who can make a decision about offering you a promotion. If there is a clear next step in the company and a vacancy is available then the only question is whether you are suitable or not. However, for many people the picture is much more complex.

If there is no clear next step, you may have to go through several discussion stages to establish whether a post can be created or whether funds have been allocated. The chances that a new post will be created or an existing post redesignated are much higher than you may think. It's the plus side of a more flexible, more reactive workplace.

Research, research

As with so many issues covered by this book, your chances of success rise in proportion to the amount of homework you do. Only begin a promotion discussion when you have enough information available on:

▌ yourself, your 'offer' and your achievements

▌ your contribution to your employer's KRAs

▌ how you can improve that contribution in a new role.

Be clear about outcomes

As with pay negotiation, don't beat about the bush. Make it clear that you are not seeking a pay review or an appraisal. Tell your boss that you want a discussion about being promoted. Don't allow yourself to be distracted from this: set an agenda and agree a time for your meeting.

Other techniques from pay negotiation that also work when seeking a promotion:

■ **Create the right impression**: work and behave as if you've already achieved promotion.

■ **Begin and end with positives**: don't make your promotion bid sound like a whingeing session.

■ **Focus on KRAs**: the company needs a strong reason to promote anybody.

■ **Don't be coercive**: if you use emotional blackmail you're forcing your employer into a win/lose situation.

■ **Think about alternative outcomes**: a chance to review the situation within a short time frame, for example. Other possibilities might be opportunities for you to handle tasks or projects that allow you to generate sufficient credibility to gain a promotion.

Make your pitch

Your opening needs to be about your contribution, and not about money. DON'T make your bid sound like a complaint. Be careful to ensure that you communicate how much you enjoy the job, particularly those parts where you have extended your job content.

You may have heard about the 'elevator pitch'. It's a term from marketing, but it is also used by recruiters. The idea is this: you arrive at a client's premises. You meet the recruiter, who takes you into the lift ('or elevator'), who puts one question to you almost in passing: 'Why do you want to work here?' The challenge is whether you make your verbal 'pitch' between the point when the lift doors close and when they open again at your destination floor (clearly you have a huge advantage if you're in a tall building!). (This idea is also creatively applied to CVs in the entertaining *Pitch Yourself: Stand Out from the CV Crowd with a Personal Elevator Pitch* by Bill Faust and Michael Faust, Financial Times/Prentice Hall, 2002.)

The elevator pitch concept works by testing clarity of thinking.

If you can justify your case for promotion in just two or three sentences, your impact is more likely to be successful. Remember that your pitch won't work if it's just about you: make sure it also says something solid about what your employer gets out of promoting you.

Working around a deferred decision

If someone else is going to be involved, and the discussion will take place in your absence (e.g. your boss is going to negotiate with the personnel department), make sure that all the evidence is included in the discussion. You should, for example, provide your boss with a written summary of all of the hard evidence behind your 'pitch'. If you put your terms in writing, sound as upbeat and reasonable as you can. Offer to go along to the meeting if it's appropriate.

Look for win/win

DO make sure that whatever you can agree is a real win/win.

In other words, it's not just a compromise, but something that takes the self-esteem of both parties seriously. You get something tangible out of the deal, so does your employer, and you part on positive terms.

'MUST DO' LIST

☑ Plan your promotion pitch very carefully. Do your homework. Track down others who have passed this way before you.

☑ Show that you fully understand your job and the organization's Key Result Areas, and provide evidence of your individual contribution.

☑ Plan your pitch as if it were an elevator pitch.

☑ Develop your relationship with your boss carefully: this person has the greatest power to assist or block your promotion.

☑ Look at the way others have fallen into career traps. Learn from their mistakes.

☑ If you're already in a rut (particularly if it's a velvet rut) take action quickly to move on. The best strategy is usually to talk to people who have moved on recently and learn from their strategy.

☑ Next time you have an appraisal, see how far you can rethink the process.

Stocking Your Lifeboat

This chapter helps you to:

▮ Spot when it's time to move out

▮ Prepare yourself for career transition

▮ Prepare your responses to the big questions

▮ Identify your motivated skills

▮ Develop your networking skills

▮ Spot your natural team role

The more I want to get something done, the less I call it work.

Richard Bach

MOVING ON

Time to quit?

If you've done everything you can to renegotiate your job and get a promotion, perhaps it's time to look at pastures new.

Recruitment training specialist Janet Basford suggests that there is a key question you should ask yourself: 'Can my existing organization offer me the next stage in my career? If yes, you need to discuss your aspirations with your company and identify how you could move to the next stage. If not, a plan then needs to be prepared looking at a goal and the strategy to bring that goal to life'.

Push and pull

There is an important rule here: you should only move on when the pull of the new opportunity or position is more powerful than the push that is propelling you away from the job you are in now. In other words, move on for the right reasons. In fact, if we only respond to the push factor ('I'll take anything, just get me out of this job'), there is a danger that we will repeat mistakes again in the next job. Focusing on the pull of the new opportunity means that you have to concentrate on what is good about the next job match: good for you, and good for the new organization.

There's an art to knowing when it's time to move on. All of the clients who tell me they are interested in job change have to face one question: 'What can you do to fix the job you're in?' This has a double effect. Firstly, people start to take control by beginning some career-related thinking; they say things like 'now I can see some light at the end of the tunnel'. Secondly, it often helps people to feel better because they start to value themselves and what they have to offer. For others there is an understandable degree of guilt at feeling that you are betraying an organization that has been home to you for a number of years. The question, however, is still the same: try to look at the possibility of renegotiating your job before you jump ship.

Before you jump ...

The rule here is simple: don't jump ship without stocking your lifeboat.

Your lifeboat contains your toolkit for a new career: your self-awareness, your career drivers, your understanding of the way that your personality fits your work, your focused 'message' (see Chapter 3).

Taking time to stock your lifeboat matters whether you're desperate to move on or reluctant to move from your present company. Without thinking ahead, you don't have a clear message about why you want to move on. Assuming that you like your present employer, you need to convince recruiters that you really do have sufficient motivation to move on. What will you do if your employer makes you some kind of counter-offer? In other words, how powerful is your impulse to change jobs, and how far have you rehearsed the real reasons for doing so? Getting your overall message right is critical.

Responses to the big questions

As soon as you feel it's time to move on you'll be interrogated by friends and family, and quickly afterwards by recruiters and employers. The hardest question to answer at this stage is 'Why?' Be prepared: you will be asked it very soon. What you say to the question 'Why do you want to move on?' will have a powerful effect on your ability to do so.

If you dislike your present situation, the risk is that your only message to recruiters is 'I hate my job'. Watch out for knee-jerk reactions if this is true. You will have very little positive to say about yourself or your last job if you have just resigned in haste. This is one reason why it is probably easier to get a job while you still have one, rather than to resign and start looking. It's nothing to do with the mechanics of job search, but it all comes down to your overall message.

Your lifeboat kit will therefore contain not only a high degree of self-awareness, but also a strong sense of what motivates you to change job.

Successful career changers know that they have to think in advance about the big questions and prepare *prepared responses*. These are short, clear and positive answers to key questions such as those outlined in Table 10.1. The emphasis is on short (each response should be about 30 seconds) and positive (don't leave any lingering problems or doubts in the questioner's mind). The useful thing about these questions is that they also help you to focus on whether you really want to move job.

Table 10.1   Prepared responses to the big questions

1. Your leaving story
   Why do you want to move on? Your response needs to be a balanced mix of positive comments about your present role and concrete reasons for wanting new opportunities.

2. How motivated are you to move?
   How settled are you in your present job? How will you feel if you have to resign?

3. What do you have to offer?
   A brief summary of who you are, what you do, and what skills and experience you have. You must be able to respond to the question 'tell me about yourself' at any time.

4. Career overview
   How can you sum up your career, in a nutshell, and make it sound both interesting and coherent?

5. Key successes
   Employers buy experience and attitude, so wrap the two up together: make your success stories communicate both your skills and your attitude to work.

6. Your style
   Be prepared to talk briefly and positively about the way you work, with colleagues, in teams and with your boss. This book will help you to focus on all three.

7. Your USP
   Your Unique Selling Point is essentially the reason why an employer might choose you over equally qualified candidates.

Who to talk to

Don't try to stock your lifeboat unassisted. Recruit others to help you to discover your strengths and plan the next steps of your journey. You may feel that you have no one to turn to. Feeling hemmed in with no options and no support is a natural reaction. Check around you, openly, and you will probably discover some allies. Possibilities will include:

▌ people in the organization who feel the same way you do

▌ people who have recently left the organization

▌ a mentor inside your organization whose advice is confidential

▌ external consultants, clients or ex-colleagues who can keep a confidence.

Don't get carried away by job search until you know where you want to go, and why. Begin with a search for information. This can be done in a way that does not become a Career-Limiting Action (see Chapter 11), by focusing on what you want to discover and not on why you want to leave. It is usually possible to find out a great deal from internal sources without clearly flagging up the fact that you are nearly ready to jump ship. Outside sources will also be helpful.

The principle here is to gather enough information before you commit to a decision that could affect the next 10 years of your life. It's exploration in two dimensions: about *you* (what you have to offer, how you work best, the kind of work you feel called to do, etc.) and about *what's out there*.

Talk to real people

Networking is a vital skill, in terms of positioning yourself for promotion, and when it comes to unlocking the question of what is available to you. We all know that, and yet most of us frantically search around for reasons not to network. It all seems a little too much like either self-promotion or begging.

'I see networking as the biggest single influencing factor whether someone is keen to get promotion within the same company or to move out,' says career coach Claire Coldwell. 'It's about knowing what you have to offer and making sure that others are aware of it too, so that when opportunities come up, you've already paved the way for a conversation. Apart from which, networking keeps you informed about what's going on and therefore keeps you interested, even at times when you may not be able to see the next move.'

10 Rules of successful networking

1. **Don't call it networking**: Come up with a description that works for you, e.g. 'fact finding', 'broadening my horizons', 'sounding people out'. When you have a term that you're happy with, tell people what you're doing.

2. **Think research, not job search**: Your questions should be about information and ideas, not 'are there any vacancies in your firm?'

3. **Step outside your comfort zone, but only just outside it**: No-one can persuade you to change from shrinking violet to networking star of the year. Find a style that works for you rather than not doing anything at all.

4. **Start with people you know**: It helps to begin by staying firmly in your comfort zone. Think carefully about the people you know who themselves know interesting people.

5. **Follow your passions**: Ask about the things that really interest you.

6. **Ask people for something they can deliver**: People generally like to help, so ask them something they can give you. Ask them:

   (a) How did you get into your line of work?

   (b) What do you enjoy about it?

   (c) What's not so great?

   (d) What's happening in your field of work?

   (e) What are the competencies of a top performer in your field?

7. **Keep the focus on the person you are talking to, not on you**: Get people to talk about themselves and they will be far more attentive.

8. **When it comes to talking about you** … Make sure you have a clear, brief message (see Chapter 6).

9. **Always seek the bounce-on**: Ask people to introduce you to others who can be equally helpful. Acknowledge the fact that you hate calling people cold, and ask a favour: 'Would you mind telephoning ahead just to say that I will be in touch?' Try to get three new contacts out of every positive meeting. If your contact runs out of ideas, ask for names of organizations and names of good recruitment consultants.

10. **Remember the fallback question**: 'Who else should I be talking to?'

How to job search without committing career suicide

A common objection to the networking concept is 'What if my employer discovers that I am seeking another job?' Think about this carefully, as this could be damaging, particularly if you decide to stay where you are in the long run.

However, we often have an irrational fear about 'what my boss will do if he finds out I'm looking somewhere else?' We expect a hurt or punitive response. Maybe we feel we are 'letting the side down' by looking over the fence. Either way, it's healthy to remember that we're all grown-ups, and people change jobs with increasing regularity.

Worrying about your employer's response can prevent you doing anything, and leave you only with the strategy of 'taking whatever comes along'. You need to look at your particular situation: what happens if your employer does discover that you are networking your way into a new job? You might be fired, but it's unlikely. More likely, life might be made difficult for you.

Don't forget that your boss and the next boss up are also keeping an eye on their prospects on the open labour market.

It really is a question of balancing your fears with the reality of what happens if you do nothing, and the danger of feeling more and more in a rut. Naturally, if your present job is vulnerable, you need to be discreet about investigating alternative jobs. This means that your networking must be focused on people who you can trust. Most recruitment consultants manage this discretion well, but they aren't necessarily the best people to help you to discover what's out there, and you do need to know what your choices are inside and outside the company. In addition, don't forget to keep your emphasis on research rather than job search, and never say anything critical about your present employer.

IDENTIFYING YOUR SKILL SET

As soon as you start talking to people you will discover the skills that they use to fulfil the roles they are in. To begin preparation for moving on, you need to take stock of your skills and learn how to communicate them to others.

Most people only have a limited idea of their skills. They tend to talk about the skills that other people have identified in them, or the skills they think they are supposed to have in order to be successful in their line of work.

Career breakthrough requires you to know something about your *motivated skills*, those skills that you use competently *and* enjoy using. How do you recognize your motivated skills? The clues are fairly clear. When you use these skills, time seems to fly by. You become absorbed in the task at hand. You feel a sense of fulfilment in what you do and the activity seems worth doing. It may even feel like fun. If this sounds unfamiliar, it could be that you haven't used your motivated skills at work for some time. Look at the things you choose to do when you are not in work, and you should see those skills fairly clearly.

However, be aware that many of us fail to see our own skills simply because we have lived with them for so long. I call them 'wallpaper skills'. After your wallpaper has been up for a few months you no longer see it, at least until somebody comments on it, and then it snaps back into focus. Many of us use high-level interpersonal skills all the time, but we have stopped seeing them. Even when others point the skills out to us, we shrug them off. We often assume (quite wrongly) that everyone else has these skills.

There are many ways of spotting your skills. Here's one of them.

▌ Divide a piece of A4 paper into three columns as in Table 10.2.

▌ Go through your work history. Job by job, list all the important activities, situations and problems. What happened as a result of your being in work?

▌ Against each identifiable action, write bullet points summarizing the context, what you did (naming the skills you used) and the outcomes you achieved.

Table 10.2 Skill analysis

Context	The skills I used	The outcome

Look at the skills you have identified and break them down into five in different categories: (1) equipment/machines, (2) people, (3) organizations, (4) information, and (5) ideas.

As you record the results in Table 10.2, what you are actually doing is composing skill stories. Stories are a great way to communicate your skills. Just as a good story is short and to the point, so your skill stories will be clear and concise. A good story has a clear beginning, middle and end, and your skill stories will have a clear three-part structure. This helps you to remember your mini-narratives and communicate them in an attention-grabbing way.

The advantage of using skill stories is that you have evidence to back up the claims you make in appraisals or job interviews. Everyone makes claims, the best performers back them up with evidence, ideally in measurable terms.

Lorraine Reynolds is PA to the MD of a German-owned healthcare company in Cheshire. Before working as a PA she was employed as a holiday rep. It was this mix of language skills and trouble-shooting that secured her a job as a PA within 5 days of returning to the UK. Lorraine used to be apologetic about working abroad, but learned how to turn the unusual into the distinctive.

Lorraine's career path has been much assisted, she says, by the ability to communicate her strengths: 'My CV today defines key personal qualities: flexibility, the diplomatic nature of the PA role, my ability to handle sensitive issues'. Lorraine has trained part-time as a life coach which, she says, helps to 'equip me to set goals for myself. You learn to focus on the parts of the job that you like, and you're able to work out problems in the job for yourself when you are not getting support.'

THE SKILLS TRIANGLE

The three-part skills story works, essentially, because you are conveying the information that employers find useful and interesting. The three parts of your story fit into the situation–contribution–result (SCR) triangle (Figure 10.1), which is a great way of remembering or recording skills.

Begin with a **situation**: a time, place and context where you used a particular skill. It doesn't have to be an earth-shattering event. Even the small stuff picks up your skill set. Next think about your individual **contribution**. What did you do? If your contribution was part of a team, what was your team role, and how effectively did you fulfil it? Finally, don't forget to record the final outcome, the **result**. Think about what key decision makers (here, or in another company) consider to be worthwhile outcomes.

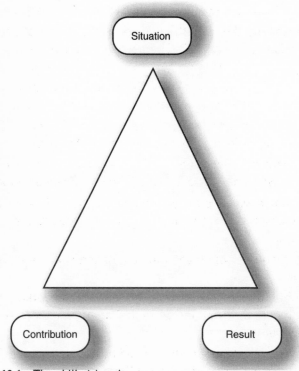

Figure 10.1   The skills triangle

ACHIEVEMENTS

One of the great spin-offs of skill identification is that you get a chance to record and communicate what you have achieved.

Try to express achievements in terms of awards, money, time or percentages if it's possible to do so.

What if you feel that you have achieved very little? This could be because you are in a job that is too narrowly focused, but it's far more likely that you have overlooked achievements. Communicating what you have to offer requires you to make *claims*, but to back up claims you need *evidence*, and the best kind of evidence of your skills is contained in defined achievements. See Table 10.3 for more details on pinning down your achievements.

Figure 10.3 Prompts to spotting your achievements

1. There was a problem or a set of obstacles, a challenge. You found some strategy for dealing with the problem: you sought help, you learned something you drew on inner resources.

2. You, personally, did something. If you did it as part of a team, concentrate on what you did personally. There was a result, something changed, something happened.

3. Try asking your colleagues and friends what differences you have made, and what you have added to organizations.

4. Go back through your work diaries and logs. Pick out occasions or projects where you made a difference.

5. Look at your job description. In what ways have you redefined your job? When have you delivered more than expectation?

6. Look at times when you invented new solutions, threw out the rule book, went the extra mile, gave 150%, brought in a key client, etc.

7. Identify moments when you turned a near-disaster into a success.

8. Remember to look at achievements in your non-working life. It's often here that you find skills that are undervalued or undeveloped.

9. Spot the times when activities would have failed, lost money or faded away if you had not been there.

A range of questions may assist in achievement spotting:

- What did I have to do to achieve this?

- What was the task or challenge?

- What did I do personally?

- What was the biggest problem?

- What was my best moment?

- What planning did I need to do?

- What obstacles did I have to overcome?

- How did I work with others?

- What action am I most proud of?

- How did I surprise myself or others?

WHAT IS YOUR NATURAL TEAM ROLE?

There are several other key steps that can build on your skills and achievements and increase your self-awareness. An important area is working out how you operate in a team.

How do you operate in teams? This is an important question in a world where nearly every CV holder claims to be a 'team player'. Identify what you bring to a team. Look at the way in which you behave most often in teams, i.e. the roles you fit into most naturally and comfortably. Exercise 10.1 helps you to identify your natural team role, but if you want to know more find an opportunity to have your team role assessed by some form of questionnaire or psychometric measure.

EXERCISE 10.1 – DISCOVERING YOUR NATURAL TEAM ROLE

Table 10.4 helps to define the way you naturally fit into a team.

Think about times when you have worked in teams. Read the statements about each team role.

Give each statement a score of 0, 1, 2 or 3 as indicated.

Table 10.4   Your natural team role

1. Ideas person			
I generally find that in teams or meetings …			
Score: 0 Hardly ever, 1 Sometimes, 2 Frequently, 3 Most or all of the time			
I come up with new ideas		I enjoy finding new ways of looking at things	
I don't feel constrained by traditional ways of doing things		I can be absorbed in my own ideas	
I am relied upon to think up solutions		I like to work out difficult problems in my head	
My perspective sometimes surprises people		I like to think 'outside the box'	
Total score			

2. Worker ant			
I generally find that in teams or meetings …			
Score: 0 Hardly ever, 1 Sometimes, 2 Frequently, 3 Most or all of the time			
I like things to be well planned and structured		I like to see how ideas can be put into practice	
I want to stop talking and start doing		I like to convert talk into action planning	
I am realistic about what will work		I prefer activity to concepts or theories	
I like to have clear goals		I am good at putting plans into practice	
Total score			

3. Progress driver			
I generally find that in teams or meetings ... **Score:** 0 Hardly ever, 1 Sometimes, 2 Frequently, 3 Most or all of the time			
I can be assertive or forceful		I am prepared to be unpopular to get results	
I am keen to get through the agenda efficiency and quickly		I am prepared to challenge others	
I tend to influence decisions or outcomes		I am keen to hit goals and targets	
I can be impatient		I am good at negotiating outcomes	
Total score			

4. Director			
I generally find that in teams or meetings ... **Score:** 0 Hardly ever, 1 Sometimes, 2 Frequently, 3 Most or all of the time			
I take charge of proceedings		I draw other people out and ask for their contribution	
I can get people to agree		I seek a view agreed by the majority	
I can persuade people to accept a decision		I remind the meeting of our objectives	
I see what team members have to offer		I often summarize or clarify what has been said by others	
Total score			

5. Explorer

I generally find that in teams or meetings ...

Score:
0 Hardly ever, 1 Sometimes, 2 Frequently, 3 Most or all of the time

I am usually enthusiastic and communicative		I can spot opportunities we can exploit	
I like to make my own contacts outside the group		I am often investigating external resources	
I suggest useful connections and contacts for others		I prefer interesting people who have something to contribute	
I am active and optimistic		I like to draw on outside ideas	
Total score			

6. Analyst

I generally find that in teams or meetings ...

Score:
0 Hardly ever, 1 Sometimes, 2 Frequently, 3 Most or all of the time

I keep calm and can think clearly		I tend to be objective and not caught up in enthusiasm	
I like to check the facts		I am good at organizing the work to be done	
I like to have supporting data		People sometimes think I am too analytical	
I enjoy analysing things		I tend to see all the options available	
Total score			

7. Consultant

I generally find that in teams or meetings ...

Score:
0 Hardly ever, 1 Sometimes, 2 Frequently, 3 Most or all of the time

I am called in to deal with particular subjects or problems		I offer skills or knowledge that are in short supply	
I am seen as an expert		I am not interested in things that I cannot make a specific contribution to	
I have specialized knowledge		I want to be useful to several groups rather than a long-term member of one group	
General discussion bores me		I want to pass on my expertise	
Total score			

8. Task master

I generally find that in teams or meetings ...

Score:
0 Hardly ever, 1 Sometimes, 2 Frequently, 3 Most or all of the time

I get things done, on deadline		I am concerned that things may go wrong	
I tend to worry about the details		I can be a perfectionist	
I remind people of deadlines		People consider me a safe pair of hands	
I spot errors in documents or plans		I can be relied upon to make things happen	
Total score			

9. Team builder			
I generally find that in teams or meetings ...			
Score: 0 Hardly ever, 1 Sometimes, 2 Frequently, 3 Most or all of the time			
I like people to get on with each other		I get on with most kinds of people	
I feel that agreement is important		I go with the majority feeling	
I support ideas that are in the common interest		I like to build up relationships between team members	
I want to get to know people better		I encourage teams to meet up socially outside work	
Total score			

Add up your total score for each box and write your top 3 team roles in Table 10.5. You may find that you have several with the same score. If so, give priority to roles where you operate proficiently *and* comfortably.

Table 10.5 My top 3 team roles

1.

2.

3.

Table 10.6 summarizes these team roles under three headings: Action, People and Thought. You may find it interesting to look back at the primary skills you identified earlier in this chapter and see how many of them fit with the team roles you have listed in Table 10.5.

Table 10.6 Three categories of team roles

Action-focused roles	Progress driver
	Worker ant
	Task master
People-focused roles	Director
	Team builder
	Explorer
Thought-focused roles	Ideas Person
	Analyst
	Consultant

Relation to Belbin types

The team roles described above should relate, roughly, to your Belbin type. The Belbin test is one of the most widely known assessments of team type and performance. For further details see www.belbin.com. To know your Belbin type, take a formal assessment using the Belbin test, and your results should be checked against the way that other people, particularly work colleagues, see you.

'MUST DO' LIST

☑   Who can you talk to in order to find out when and how to move on?

☑   Record your primary skills. Try communicating skill stories during your next appraisal.

☑   What skills do you perform at a high level? What skills do you enjoy using? How many of these skills are you able to use in your present job?

☑   What have been your biggest achievements during the past 12 months?

☑   Check out your natural team roles. How often do you get a chance to perform in these roles?

The JLA Skill Cards

Both this book and *How To Get A Job You'll Love* outline a range of techniques for identifying your motivated skills. There is another tool available: the JLA Skill Card Sort, designed to spot your primary skills and show you how to communicate them to decision makers. The Skill Cards come with a full set of instructions for use in career development.

See www.johnleescareers.com for further details.

Making Your Mark in a New Job

This chapter helps you to:

❚ Build your job from the offer stage

❚ Use the critical stages in your new position to assist career development

❚ Seek quick wins

❚ Avoid Career-Limiting Actions

❚ Begin to position yourself for promotion

I don't know anything of luck. I've never banked on it, and I'm afraid of people who do. Luck to me is something else; hard work and realizing what is opportunity and what isn't.

Lucille Ball

ACCEPTING THE JOB

It's healthy to take one step back in the process of taking a new job by looking at what you can do to negotiate the job content before you start. Sounds unlikely? Think again. You have far more possibility of affecting job content at the point of accepting a job offer than you probably will have for the first 2 years of employment.

The point when you receive a job offer is critical. It's a time when, for a brief moment, you have some leverage over a number of elements:

▐ Your **salary**: this should only be negotiated when an employer has come to the firm decision to appoint you.

▐ Other aspects of your **financial package**: pensions, medical insurance, etc.; whatever is important to you.

▐ Any **other aspects**: you may be able, for example, to negotiate longer holidays or flexible working arrangements.

▐ **Job content**: by making your employer a positive 'offer' you will be able to exert some influence, however small, over job content.

These ideas need some unpacking because, at first sight, they may seem either idealistic, or possibly only something that very confident senior candidates can achieve. Not so. As we have seen, any job is a 'deal' between employer and worker, it's just a matter of whether you realize what cards you hold. Trying to negotiate any of these points before the job offer stage is a bad idea, because it can give an employer a reason not to appoint you. Resist the temptation to discuss anything in the package until you hold an offer (with the possible exception of job content, which you can ask about at interview in order to demonstrate your interest). Once an employer has fallen in love with you, you're playing by different rules: a trip has been switched in the employer's mind, and now they're worried that you won't accept. Be aware of the opportunity cost of their having to go back to the market and seek new candidates.

However, do be aware that you can't negotiate on everything. Stick to the aspects that matter most to you. In terms of planning your future, the best strategy if the money is acceptable is to focus on the job itself. Be careful: what you don't want to do is sound as if you are complaining and you don't really want the job. Always begin and end any comment on job content with a positive comment; for example, 'Let me begin by saying how exciting this job opportunity is for me. There are just one or two things I need to discuss with you before I accept. The good news is it's not the money! What I'd like to do is to ask you to think about restructuring the role to increase the amount of training I'll be doing. If you remember, at interview we discussed how important this is to me. Now I'd like to suggest two things that will benefit the company … '.

A fall-back strategy is to ask for a chance to begin certain activities within a certain time frame: 'OK, so how about if I'm given a chance to run my own accounts within 6 months or so?'

If you'd rather run a mile than make any kind of counter-offer before beginning a job, just think what you're throwing away: the chance to shape the job from the outset. Negotiating the job content is both good for you and good for the organization, and it can make the difference between early promotion and career blocks.

Finally, if you're still struggling with the idea, try for one thing. Look at what you think may be the difference between the job on offer and the job you'd really like to do, and ask for one thing to be changed. 'Thanks for the offer. I'm delighted. There's just one thing I'd like you to consider before I accept. I'd like a chance to do more … in the job. If we can fix that, I'll be on board!' As long as you begin and end your comment on a positive note, you've a high chance that it will happen.

BEGINNING A NEW JOB

Your path to promotion begins in your first week in the job.

Your first strategy is to listen, learn and ask intelligent questions. Find out who the key people are in the organization, the people who will make decisions about your future. But first of all start by identifying two kinds of people:

▌ People who are visibly doing a good job. These people will eventually be good people to talk to, but for the moment just watch and learn.

■ People who are **information brokers** within the organization: the people who know where things are, who does what, and who to ask questions. Hunt around, these people exist in every organization. Sometimes it's the Managing Director's PA, sometimes it's the security guard on reception.

DOING YOUR HOMEWORK

Just as your research into the company got you the job in the first place, learning to identify the major problems and headaches within your organization will give you vital clues about what needs to be done to create success. Try to spot your 'homework': company information you can take home and absorb, so you can learn about products, initiatives, supply chain, customer contacts, and so on.

Keep a notebook. Write down names, procedures and contact numbers. Learn the names of key people. Spot the people who can make your job easier, or can make it hell. Try not to step on toes at this stage: first impressions matter, and you don't want inadvertently to make life enemies now. If the stationery department will only issue you a notepad on a Tuesday between 2 and 3 pm, run with it. Making waves now could be a serious Career-Limiting Action (see below), because people are making their minds up about you.

LEARNING THE JOB – QUICKLY

Ask what's expected of you and which benchmarks you will be up against fairly soon. Discover the cycle of routine activities: there's nothing worse than being totally unprepared for an end-of-month report, or being criticized within 2 weeks of starting for not supplying key information to your boss.

Learn as much as you can about policies, procedures and standards – the rules. Conformity may be boring, but it keeps you out of trouble in your first few weeks. It also signals your ability to learn systems quickly, which is a useful transferable skill. Conformity in new recruits is highly valued because you quickly transform yourself from problem to asset, and you start to look as if you really belong.

Work out the key tasks of your job, how you do things. Pay particular attention to the amount of authority you need to obtain to do or buy anything.

When learning, observe and listen, and ask only intelligent questions. Don't expect to be spoon-fed. If you really don't understand a process or task, find someone at your level or a junior level to explain it to you step by step rather than take up a manager's time.

Be careful how far you suggest good ideas at this stage. The basic rule is: don't criticize and don't run down the way someone is doing the job now. However, you may be able to make some tentative suggestions of new things that can be done. This is best done on a sharing basis ('Perhaps we could have a chat some time about that') rather than telling people how things should be done. Often it's best to sit on your reactions to how things are done, and just focus at this stage on enthusiasm for the job as it stands, throwing in a few additional ideas that add value to the present process rather than challenge it.

If you spot something that appears to be done inefficiently, make a note but don't comment just yet (see the section on quick wins below). Commenting immediately marks you out as a Smart Alec and a threat, and people will start to be less open.

WORKING ON THE PEOPLE DIMENSION

Don't rely just on your day one grand tour to meet new people. Try to sit next to new colleagues every day at lunch or at coffee. Seize opportunities to visit other departments or branches. When introduced to new colleagues don't just smile and nod; show interest in their jobs and problems, and show you are impressed by what they do. You may be the first person who has really listened to them talk about their jobs for a while. Keep a note of their names and their areas of responsibility. If you're stuck, they will usually respond to a phone call along the lines of 'I'm new here – help me out'.

READING HOW YOUR COMPANY CULTURE VIEWS PROMOTION

Something you need to learn early on in the game is how your company views activity that may be viewed as promotion seeking. Be aware, of course, that this can be subjective: what is promotion seeking to one person is simply 'doing a good job' to another. There is no such thing as work activity that is not in some way related to promotion (or at least, retention); you're either undertaking activity that encourages your employer to keep you and develop you, or you're committing Career-Limiting Actions. Contrary to popular belief, there's no real middle ground. The favourite strategy of 'getting on with the job' is far from neutral.

Employment consultant Peter Jackson suggests that 'the difficulty is that each company has a different culture in terms of attitudes to promotion, with the US style of organization expecting people to put themselves forward for promotion, compared with the British ethos of "waiting till you're selected" otherwise you might appear to be pushy'. Peter's insight demonstrates a spectrum of possibilities between passive and active. The difficulty is that in the twenty-first century there are fewer and fewer companies who are prepared to manage our careers for us. The 'wait and hope' strategy works reasonably well in a paternalistic system, but as each year goes by there are fewer organizations in the UK that work that way. For good or ill, we are moving towards an economy that requires an active approach to career management or, as this book suggests, *career awareness* (see Chapter 3).

Career awareness in this context goes right back to the primary finding of our research: that career development is about being aware of yourself and deeply aware of organizational reality. In this case, an active approach hunts down information about how far your organization accepts and values behaviours that are clear signals of potential. Each organization has its own style and its own limits. Using your first few months in the company to find out just this will be time well spent.

Have your finger on the pulse of your company, and work out how things really work there. Don't assume that your new employer will behave like others you have worked for, or like organizations where your friends work. What works in one organization doesn't always work in another. This can be problematic for someone who changes companies and brings to the new culture an attitude to promotion that doesn't travel well.

As you become established, it is time to use strategies outlined in Chapter 2 of this book. Take the advice of Robin Wood, MD of outplacement specialists CMC, who reminds us that you attract the attention of managers by being 'positive, can do, energetic, cheerful, enthusiastic and always prepared to go above and beyond the call of duty.'

LOOKING FOR QUICK WINS

If you want to make a rapid impact in a new role, look for rapid results. Ask around: what gets in the way of productivity? What can be resolved obviously and cheaply? Unsuccessful managers often fail because they try to impose a template or an idea on an organization without investigating how it already works, or doesn't. Managers who seek quick wins often talk to people on the shopfloor, particularly those who are customer facing, and ask 'What could we do better?' and 'What are we missing?' The answers are often enlightening. Staff in customer-facing jobs often have very clear ideas of what goes wrong. They will frequently say things like 'I've told the management, but … '. Pick out one or two of these, check whether the problem and solution are real, and move ahead; but don't forget to give praise and credit to the person who gave you the idea.

Ask your colleagues what gets in the way of organizational success, and seek permission to implement two or three changes that are low on cost and high on imagination. Make sure you follow up: don't be a one-hit wonder.

LOOKING FOR LEVERAGE

You have a finite amount of energy, so working longer hours and harder can only produce limited results. If you really want to work smarter, not harder, focus on the projects that make the biggest difference and have the biggest impact.

The next step, once you start to become established, is described by occupational psychologist Derek Wilkie: 'Identify an area of work that is currently or will be a strategic focus for the organization and demonstrate competence, or make progress in working towards the strategic objective. (There is an element of luck here in "catching the wave" – we can't develop competence overnight.)'

This helpful advice contains some key ideas. First of all, as indicated in Chapter 5, you need to identify anything that looks like a strategic focus; in other words, a Key Result Area. 'Catching the wave' is often about tuning in to the major concerns, if not obsessions, of key decision makers. Derek Wilkie adds: 'Identify who is influential in the organization and find ways of working with them (often quite easy as these people often start initiatives and seek people who are keen to help them achieve them, regardless of organizational hierarchy). Achieve a major new project/initiative/goal. Seek the advice of an internal mentor (formal or informal).'

NEW BOSS, NEW YOU

Changes of senior staff are frequent. If you get a new boss, see it as an opportunity to try a new approach. Do more of the things you do well and enthusiastically, and ask to delegate some tasks that you find less interesting. Offer solutions, not problems, and you will make an impression quickly. Look at the work you do as a series of projects. What is your involvement in each project, and how can you increase it? Build up a portfolio of your successes, and make sure they are known in the organization.

CAREER-LIMITING ACTIONS

In Chapter 1 we reviewed the factors that make you promotable. As you become more attuned to your organization you should also become more aware of the activities and behaviours that have the reverse effect.

Look around you at your colleagues who complain about their lack of progression, and see how many of them are demonstrating Career-Limiting Actions (Table 11.1). You might like to look, honestly, to see how many of them are true for you.

Table 11.1   Career-Limiting Actions (CLAs)

Tasks	DON'T limit yourself to your job description unless your aim is to irritate.
	DON'T double-check every detail with your boss. Work out the things you do need to check, and gradually broaden the tasks where you are able to take the initiative.
	DON'T go to your boss with problems every time a task is delegated to you. Offer solutions, and check resources and likely snags when the delegation takes place.

People	DON'T be overcompetitive. Being competitive is fine, but climbing over the backs of others to reach your personal goals is widely resented.
	DON'T gossip and criticize. It may make you entertaining in coffee breaks, but doesn't position you as someone who can be trusted to bring out the best in others.
	DON'T hog the credit. Share it. Make sure your boss knows who else is working well. If your boss wants the credit, live with that sometimes.
	DON'T fail to delegate. Ideally, you should be training up your successor.
Your boss	DON'T fail to observe your boss's style. Don't just do what your boss wants, but do it in the way he or she wants it done. See Table 9.2 for more details.
	DON'T ignore your boss's goals. As our survey pointed out, working in tune with your boss's goals is a great career plus. Blocking them is the perfect CLA.
	DON'T invade your boss's win time. Your boss, like you, has time stealers (see Chapter 5) – don't become one. Invade when you must, not when you feel like it. Plan your contact time with your boss carefully and make the most of it. See the 20/5 principle in Chapter 9.
	DON'T feed your boss's pet hates. Tidy that desk, or pick the phone up after three rings. Work out what really irritates your boss and stop doing it. It's worth the personal struggle and allows you to negotiate over things that really matter.
	DON'T get out of touch with your industry. Happily admitting that you are no longer up to date and using phrases like 'in my time ... ' clearly marks you as disposable goods.

Continued

	DON'T forget the stuff your boss values, whether it's telephone numbers or the names of her children.
Processes	DON'T put too much or too little in writing. Each organization has its own internal rules on memos/emails confirming decisions. Learn what is acceptable and necessary, and always do it with a light touch rather than sounding bossy.
	DON'T fight the bureaucrats. Upsetting those people who want you to fill in Form H76T by Wednesday only adds to negative messages about you. Fill the form in, and move on.
	DON'T hold long and unnecessary meetings. People love short, focused meetings, and rarely get them.
Attitudes and behaviours	DON'T dress like a walking CLA. Dress like the next grade up, not like someone 2 weeks from retirement.
	DON'T say NO to everything. Learn to say no, but as positively as you can. Don't say 'no' just out of instinct.
	DON'T say YES to everything. Overcommitting leads to underperformance, and gives you the reputation of someone who doesn't deliver.
	DON'T take your moods to work. Try to maintain a reasonably consistent, friendly style. Smile. It helps.
	DON'T fail to keep connections open both within and outside the organization.
	DON'T misread your organization's attitude to promotion. Making the assumption that your employer encourages overt promotion-seeking behaviour may be a major CLA.
	DON'T take criticism or rejection personally. New ideas get shot down all the time. Learn to bounce back.

DON'T take yourself too seriously.

DON'T communicate badly, whether verbally or in writing. Take care to speak and write accurately and without glaring errors.

POSITIONING YOURSELF FOR A PROMOTION

'Don't think of promotion as the target', suggests outplacement specialist Ron Feasey. For him the question is rather 'How can I make a bigger contribution to the organization and/or how can I widen my experience? Overt career ambition can turn off managers.'

Lining yourself up for promotion is a subtle task. It's about both reality and perception. The reality may be that you're understimulated by your present role and ready for promotion. However, your manager may have a completely different picture. The *perception* may be that you are happy doing what you are doing, and the best strategy is to leave you alone. Even worse, you may have made some mistakes recently because you no longer find that the role demands your full attention. Your manager may interpret the mistakes as 'unready for promotion' rather than 'losing interest because the job is over-familiar'.

Individuals can also make an impact or show initiative in companies where they are not working at the moment. Harry Freedman runs Career Energy in London, but his turning point in the past was when he attended a meeting of a not-for-profit organization: 'I felt the discussion at the meeting was some-what unstructured and unproductive so the next day I wrote to the organizers with my view of how I thought they could best achieve their aims. They came straight back, and asked me to develop my thinking. They raised funds on the back of my proposal and offered me the job of Chief Executive, which I held for 7 years.'

PROMOTION AS NEGOTIATION

When you are offered a promotion (or your job is restructured to your advantage, which may be better for you than a promotion), you have rather less chance than at the job offer stage of negotiating every aspect of the job. The reason for this is that your employer feels no great sense of risk that you will go elsewhere; after all, they're offering you a promotion, aren't they? You don't have the same leverage as at the job offer stage, which is why you will need to work harder if you think you have some chance of turning a good job into a great one.

Fall-back is on the appraisal techniques outlined in Chapter 9. In other words, you need to think about carefully composing a win/win offer.

Some principles are exactly parallel to job offer, however:

1. Never accept without taking time for reflection, but always make your response positive: 'That's brilliant. There's obviously a lot to think about. Would you mind if I kick some ideas around and come back to you in a day or two? But may I say thanks very much for your confidence in me.'

2. Even when a promotion is offered out of the blue, you have some say over job content.

3. You may also have some possibility to influence other aspects, such as the financial package. If you have any leverage, however, it's far better to concentrate on job content and the challenges of the job. If you get that one right, the money should follow.

See also the specific strategies for outlining a promotion outlined in Chapter 9.

'MUST DO' LIST

☑ Begin to shape your job even from the job offer stage.

☑ Work at the first steps you take in your next job.

☑ Who are the information brokers in your organization? How can you get them on your side?

☑ What quick wins can you achieve in your present position?

☑ How well do you read your new employer's attitude in terms of promotion seeking?

Breaks and Switches

This chapter helps you to:

▌ Consider alternatives to conventional careers

▌ Look seriously at growth, career breaks and retraining

▌ Build your career in small increments

▌ Seek an integrated life

Most people are about as happy as they make up their mind to be.

Abraham Lincoln

PREPARING FOR A LIFE OF CAREER CHANGE?

Alternatives to promotion

When you are thinking about your next step, particularly if that step might be outside the organization, take account of the fact that there is more than one way of looking at career progression. Don't accept that the only way of having a career is to move endlessly upwards from one promotion to the next.

There is evidence from a variety of research that career change is becoming more commonplace. This is not just job change, but a change of sector. In the USA, for example, it is now commonly accepted that most people change careers at least three times during a working lifetime. In fact, there are those who argue very strongly that we only have one 'career', but it has different dimensions to it (including learning, career breaks and family time); for example, careers researcher Sara Bosley: 'By career I mean a sequence of jobs and job-related experiences, rather than the more commonly used meaning which implies increasing responsibility, status and income.' In other words, there is far more than one way of having and enjoying a career.

Research on career change and career breaks

In mid-2003 cahoot, the Internet bank, conducted an opinion poll focused on career change. The results tell us some interesting things about how and why people change careers. Table 12.1 lists some of the key findings.

Table 12.1   Feedback from the cahoot Career Progressive Survey 2003

Career change

▪ On average, people expected to change career three times in a working lifetime and 13% of those surveyed expected to change careers five times or more.

▪ People spent on average between 2 and 5 years at a company before moving on, however, 14% admitted to staying with a company for just 1–2 years.

▪ Women were twice as likely as men to stay for a shorter period of 1 or 2 years.

▪ People aged 35 or over were most likely to have stayed at a company for 5 years or more.

▪ Those aged 25–34 had a much higher expectation of changing career in their working lifetime compared with those aged 55 and over.

▪ Almost one-quarter (22%) had changed their career because they were bored and needed a change. A further 10% needed to find a better work/life balance. 9% felt that their previous career did not pay enough.

Continued

Career breaks

▌ Over a quarter (27%) had either already taken an extended career break or planned to do so at some stage.

▌ Over half of those surveyed (51%) said that they would love to take an extended break but couldn't afford to.

Retraining for a new career

▌ On average, people estimated that it would cost between £500 and £1000 to retrain for a new career, with one in 10 (10%) estimating that it would cost over £5000.

▌ Almost three-quarters (72%) said that they have not changed their career because they can't afford to, yet 89% of those surveyed were not completely satisfied with their current career and salary/package.

Dream jobs

▌ Almost one-quarter (23%) said that their dream career move would be to become a writer, 11% said they would like to be in the movies and just 2% said they would like to be a politician.

Career drivers

▌ Personal satisfaction was the most important factor in a career and salary was the least important. There was no significant gender, age or regional difference in this finding.

Job security

▌ 84% of people surveyed felt some degree of insecurity in their current job.

▌ People aged 35–44 were the most likely to feel completely secure in their job (18%).

Reproduced with the permission of cahoot, the Internet bank from Abbey National.

Retraining: barrier or gateway?

The most significant finding of the cahoot survey appears to relate to money: most people believe that money is not their primary motivator (see Chapter 4), but money is seen as the main block preventing a move into a new career.

One of the reasons behind this survey was an interest in how far people would like to change their career or take a break, and it was interesting to see that a considerable number of people estimate the cost of retraining as being as high as £5000. More realistically, most estimate that retraining will cost between £500 and £1000: the cost of a good-quality wide-screen television or a week's holiday. Clearly the idea of retraining is more expensive than the reality.

In practice, there are many different options for retraining, many of them extremely low cost. Instead of doing a full-blown MBA, for example, you can often follow short courses in particular subjects, but at the same level. There are many options for online or distance learning. Your bookshop or local library has a huge amount of learning resources available in book form. If you find it tedious absorbing information from long books, there are many publications now that encapsulate information in brief, giving you bullet-point summaries of everything from management theory to website design. The world is awash with free learning opportunities.

Another option, of course, is to negotiate learning opportunities at work – either in your present job or in your next one. Consider learning as part of your benefits package; negotiate both learning and training experiences (which can range from sponsored study to training events, and can also include broadening your range of work experiences). Make sure that you get your employer to be as specific about the learning benefits of the job (e.g. committing training opportunities to paper after an appraisal) as you would be if they were financial benefits.

Changing occupations

The cahoot opinion poll provides several findings that relate to several themes of this book, but particularly in terms of the areas of career change. It is interesting, for example, how many people would enjoy the prospect of a career break or would positively like to move into a new field of work.

People are becoming more conscious of the possibility of a career that involves at least one occupational shift, and probably involves some retraining or new learning. We have choices to make, and the more aware we can become, the better our decisions in terms of investing in ourselves and choosing what to do next.

Career breaks

Some employers still give their staff sabbatical leave, to study, to travel, to refresh themselves. These breaks sometimes send people back to work renewed, and at other times prompt a career change.

However, for many, the idea of a career break (taken out of choice rather than necessity) seems an unaffordable luxury or a pipe dream. It's interesting, then, to see that the opinion poll referred to above suggested that nearly one-third of respondents had enjoyed an extended career break or were planning to have one.

The Judao-Christian tradition of the Sabbath reflects the idea that all work needs to pause, and all workers need to recharge their batteries. The 24/7 economy increasingly reduces the time we have to do this. The need for breaks is more important than ever. Ultimately, it's about your choices, and your overall balance of learning, living and working. However, it's important to include the idea of career breaks as part of the larger questions about why you want to be promoted and how you want to spend your working life. When it comes to negotiating your 'offer' with your employer, past or future, remember that *the time when you are not working* can become part of the deal – time for doing more of the things you outlined in Exercise 7.1.

Career breakthrough by small increments

You may have picked up this book or *How To Get A Job You'll Love* with the idea that within you, somewhere, is a hidden 'real' you, a secret self that can be unlocked by asking the right questions or reading the right books. Many self-help books are written along these lines. Recently, a number of people have challenged the 'hidden self' idea, suggesting that we have multiple, alternative 'selves'.

If you have spent all your working life working in complex bureaucracies, you may know as a matter of certainty that you want to break out and do something different. It may be attractive to believe that you have a single, concealed 'dream' career, rather like the Monty Python accountant who always wanted to be a lumberjack. Occasionally you do meet people who have a very clear dream job. Many feel as if they *ought* to have an ideal job, and envy those who do, without realizing how demanding life is for those people who know that they really only have one choice if they want to avoid saying 'I wish … ' for the rest of their lives.

The vast majority of us have a much more undefined sense of what we would 'really' like to do. For some, the lack of definition provides a great excuse – to do nothing. We're trained by our upbringing to seek clear outcomes and work hard at achieving them. We're not very good at 'What if?'

The idea of multiple career routes helps, because instead of having one fixed idea you have a cluster of related possibilities. Now you're closer to career awareness (see Chapter 3).

Let's take Daniel as an example. He has spent all his career so far in accountancy roles, and now he is juggling a number of career ideas including charity work, public-sector work for a housing association and working as a small business adviser, while at the same time he is very attracted by a commercial role in a large company. How does Daniel make sense of his options? Does he need to make a move?

One answer to this question is for Daniel to make more of the exploration zone in his job (see Table 4.2), which is what he did. He created time to meet people in some of the work sectors that interested him. He persuaded his company to allow him to work much more closely with senior operations staff to get a 'feel' for the cutting edge of the business. Outside work he is working as a voluntary small business advisor with the Prince's Trust, and about to contribute to a housing project through his local church.

Making a huge leap in your career is not straightforward. This is particularly true if this involves a change of field (e.g. moving from marketing to photography) or a major change of lifestyle (e.g. from financial director to author). It's a risky process because it's about moving from known to unknown. However, the risk will often be magnified by those who gleefully tell us 'I know someone who tried that ... they're broke now.' It's easy to turn these exploratory thoughts into a game of 'win or bust'. If you play by those rules, you either risk everything or do nothing.

The idea that we can change careers by gradual steps can be helpful for many, particularly because this kind of change can involve juggling a huge number of variables. We may find that we move forward more effectively if we attempt experimental steps, mini-rehearsals, trying on a number of roles to see whether they fit. There are many examples of people who have gradually built new careers on this basis, by flexing the job they are in, taking on new roles in the experimental zone of work, and using their leisure time to experiment with learning prospects or business ideas. Herminia Ibarra's excellent book *Working Identities* (Harvard Business Books, 2003) explores these issues in a fascinating discussion.

Integrity in work

The whole direction of this book is to give you the tools to understand your organization and those who manage you, to develop a range of skills and tools, but above all to understand yourself, and why you work. Moving onwards and upwards is about working out what *you* have to offer and communicating that in the best way you can, and so it certainly shouldn't be about becoming somebody different. As the discussion on individuation in Chapter 7 made clear, our ultimate goal may be about living a complete life: a career of integrity. Integrity is a perfect word here, because it captures a sense of doing things that are true to the way we are, and a sense of wholeness and well-being. Getting promoted is only a means, not an end.

Bill Walmsley, Business Development Director of CERTT, reminds you to 'Be true to yourself – it's no fun getting promoted and finding yourself a square peg in a round hole.'

So, for those of you who have got this far in the book and are still saying 'do I really want a promotion?' – you're asking the right question. If you do, and it provides you with a job that feels more complete, more stimulating and more *you* than the role you're in, then go for it. Use the tools presented here to create the right opportunity. And if you're still unsure, then maybe you need to look more carefully at redesigning the job you're in (and getting paid the right amount for it), or other issues such as learning, life balance, a career break or changing your job completely.

Ultimately, your pathway to promotion and success will be most fruitful if it is about job fulfilment; about finding the right promotion, not just a promotion; about learning to negotiate opportunities that are a great match for your personality, skills, know-how and motivation. Ultimately, it's about *integration*; about moving to a point in life where you find your life experience and aspirations run in parallel: finding something close to what makes you a balanced, integrated individual.

The pitcher cries for water to carry
and a person for work that is real.

Marge Piercy (from *'Circles on the Water'*)

'MUST DO' LIST

☑ Is the next step for you promotion or career development, or both?

☑ How can you begin to explore some of the wider choices that will shape your longer term career?

☑ What training or learning opportunities can you negotiate or create for yourself?

☑ Talk to others about the 'What if?' possibilities for your career. What experimental next steps can you take?

☑ If enjoying your job was a criminal offence, *would there be enough evidence to convict you*?

Steps Towards the Perfect Promotion

This chapter helps you to:

▋ Take on board top tips from experienced managers and coaches

▋ Focus on your next steps

▋ Put together a career development plan for the next 6 months

Tomorrow is often the busiest day of the week

Spanish proverb

STEPPING FORWARD

Chapter 2 outlined the research with senior managers that underpins this book. The responses to the final question, 'What one piece of advice would you give to someone who wants to achieve a promotion at work in the next 12 months?' prompted so many useful responses that it seems appropriate to record several of them here. Some of them are inspirational, some practical, many contradict each other. One respondent gave a healthy warning: 'I think there's a danger in offering people one-liners that have been successful for others unless you add the caveat about not expecting the experience of others necessarily to work for you'. The following therefore represents a miscellany of good ideas. One, or a combination of several, could be your next step:

▮ Fulfil your specified role in such a way that your managers are more than satisfied by your all round contribution and your colleagues would support your promotion. (Rod Howgate, founding partner of recruitment consultancy Howgate Sable)

▮ Know the business, where the important pieces of work that have the greatest impact are taking place and move towards developing knowledge in those areas. (Breda O'Toole, HR professional)

▮ Define what you can do for the business, build relationships with those who can help you do what you do best, find opportunities for exposure in your area of competence. (Andrew Bramley, careers and training specialist, South Africa)

▮ Be a generalist rather than a specialist in your field. Providing you have strong communication and leadership skills a little knowledge of a lot of subjects goes farther than in-depth knowledge of a narrow business base. (Mike Wallwork, Communications Director)

▮ Focus on key drivers that you can influence and will directly link to the senior people you aspire to join, e.g. customer satisfaction, sales targets, revenue and cost reduction. (Stuart Carter, coaching specialist)

▮ Decide on a plan of action and stick to it. Ensure your boss knows what your immediate ambitions are. (Stephen Hunter, Commercial and NHS Trust Board Chairman)

▮ Tell people how well you are doing! Raise your profile by clear and consistent communication. (Andrew Carr, recruitment trainer)

▮ Be seen to put the company's needs first, volunteering for assignments and projects and then working like hell in a highly visible manner to deliver (Robin Wood, MD of Career Management Consultants Limited. (CMC))

▮ It is a tough world at the moment and increasingly competitive. It is therefore vital to make an impression. Build relationships with the right people in the organization and demonstrate that you can get on with anyone you work with. Also be prepared to show a genuine interest/dedication to your chosen career. Put in 'extra' in your own time, it might be unpaid financially, but it is an investment for the future. I believe opportunities for personal development should be seen as a 'reward' in themselves. Consider where you want to be next and start and understand the processes attached to that new role – moving from a specialist to more of a generalist. (Anne Stojic, HR consultant)

▎ Be very clear about what it is you want, and why you want it. Then make sure that your reasons are valid. Where does it fit into your longer term career plan? What would it add to your CV? What are the possible implications on your home life/family? (Beverley Gartside, life coach)

▎ Develop a model of ideal knowledge, skill and behaviour for the next step on the promotional ladder and if the model fits with your career hopes and aspirations use it as a developmental tool. (Ian Webb, HR director)

▎ Ask people who are in positions of influence what types of things they look for in people 'with potential'. Take care of your current job and do it well. Show interest in your own development and create good relationships with peers and managers. (Andy Cole, HR & training consultant)

▎ Do the current job so well that people entrust you with more than the job content. (John Courtis, Director of search and selection firm Courtis and Partners Ltd)

▎ Make yourself visible to the people who have the power to promote. This can be done in a number of ways, but informal contact, that is, really getting to know the people in power will help a person get promoted. Also, it is important to be seen in a positive light, and this can be achieved by doing one's work well; doing more than is necessary; taking the initiative in some way in the organization. (Garth Toombs, Canadian outplacement/ careers specialist)

▎ Work 'smartly' hard. Do nothing that does not or cannot leverage greater results. Use your resources very wisely. Treat every employee and customer with the highest of respect and integrity. Focus on the creation of new opportunities as opposed to spending time of expense management. Get new revenue streams to grow profitably fast. Head for the top priority revenue streams to get noticed as a doer where it matters. Surround yourself with great people and let them get the glory of the results generated by your leadership. (Marc J. Beaulieu, insurance broker, California)

▌ Change jobs if you what you are doing isn't something you enjoy and would do for less money or free. Get a job where your talents shine without it looking like brain surgery. (Pegi Wheatley, staffing consultant, San Francisco)

▌ Spend 100% of your time doing an excellent job, and another 50% of your time making sure everybody who matters know what a good job you are doing; i.e. you may have to neglect family, hobbies, etc., and become a workaholic; above all you really must want that promotion and the sacrifices it entails. (John Eardley, outplacement consultant)

▌ I think that companies increasingly look to the outside world for senior positions – they seem to have more faith in those they don't know well than those they do. Against that, people who want to get promoted need to take an outside in view, as well as an inside out one – the danger is they get taken for granted and passed over. You need to work out what problem your boss has (the deep down one) and provide a solution for that – without becoming a threat to him. (Philip Spencer, consumer marketing expert)

▌ Raise your level of thinking to that of the role sought. There is no point trying to become a director if you are still thinking like a manager; and no point trying to become a leader of people if your thinking is that of a foot soldier! (Bernard Pearce, HR and careers consultant)

▌ Communicate well. It has to be known that you are delivering without stuffing your performance down people's throats. (Alan Small, outplacement consultant)

▌ Winning the argument is not always the best solution to some situations. Presenting 'options' and 'potential solutions' demonstrates a willingness to take responsibility to help solve problems and think creatively towards supporting other members of the team. (Deirdre Hughes, Director, Centre for Guidance Studies, University of Derby)

▌ Be very clear on why you are doing this (money is never a consistent factor), what you will bring to the new position and how you would benefit the company in this new position. Don't forget how this new position will impact on your personal life (bring loved ones on board). Be aware that a position of responsibility may be isolating and distance you from some former friends – are you ready for this? (Andrée Harper, occupational psychologist)

▌ Talk to someone who can promote you about what you want and find out what they want from you. (June Burrough, Director, The Pierian Centre)

▌ Learn about the area you are interested in, for example by shadowing or offering to help (voluntarily) if appropriate. Develop the appropriate skills and demonstrate them (e.g. through undertaking developmental tasks) to those with influence or responsibility for opportunities in that area of work. Express enthusiasm to learn skills/develop knowledge you are lacking. (Sara Bosley, careers researcher)

▌ Develop a strategy to achieve it; develop a strategy if you don't. Either way, follow through. (Melissa Rosati, Editorial & Production Director, McGraw-Hill UK)

▌ Look at your role and the organization as a whole – what can be improved upon, implemented and have a direct result to the success of the company? What will you be remembered for? (Justine Wilkinson, IT recruitment consultant)

▌ Four steps to success:

1. Know what you want and why within the next 3 months max.

2. Tell personnel or your management soon the outcome of (1).

3. Make sure you have a safe pair of hands in your present job – you are unlikely to be given something more valuable to do if you are not looking after well what you have now.

4. See if what you want is available outside of your present company, don't be afraid to move outside to get what you want if your current employer cannot give it.

(Rob Head, formerly Corporate Development Manager, Octel Corp.).

YOUR 10-STEP PROGRAMME

The following steps build on the key areas of this book and draw on the above summary of what is most likely to be successful as your next move.

Step 1: Invest in yourself

Put time aside to review, plan and investigate possibilities for your future. Think of yourself as a solo company. If a company is going downhill it needs to look carefully at its products and services. You, too, can do something similar if you feel you're not making progress. Act as if you were the biggest shareholder in 'Me Plc' – that way you will see the benefits of a regular progress check. Spend at least one day a quarter focusing on your job, cataloguing your successes and looking at areas where you can add to your learning. It also helps you to stock your lifeboat in case you need to jump ship.

Step 2: Know the organization

As we've discussed, there's no point focusing on your own strengths unless you know what the organization needs. Think about your organization's headaches, worries, opportunities and goals. Use the checklist in Chapter 5 to spot the gaps you have in your organizational knowledge. Find out as much as you can using your own resources; imagine all your life savings were about to be invested in this organization and look at it accordingly. Find out who the key information brokers are within the organization. Most people operate largely in the dark, but there will be key people who know virtually everything and everyone.

Step 3: Watch the politics

This is a key survival activity: organizational survivors are often not those with the best skills, but those who are most keenly tuned to office politics. The ones who become discarded are all too often the people who can't read the writing on the wall. Understand what your boss really wants in life, and help to provide it. Be very careful around new bosses: re-establish your presence just as if you were starting a new job.

Step 4: Be an ideas machine

Don't be blinkered by your own industry sector. Beg, steal or borrow great ideas from other environments. Keep up to date: read widely, hunt down useful contacts, go to exhibitions and conferences. Become hungry for new information about your sector and about your client base, and keep people informed that you are doing so. Collate and summarize key information; be seen as an information broker. Setting up an e-group (Yahoo and Hotmail offer simple solutions) around a particular subject is easy, free, and gets results – it enables a group of people with a common interest to share ideas and post questions. It's no substitute for face-to-face networking, but it can help you to expand your range of contacts.

Step 5: Adopt a strategy for rejection

Even the best sales performers get a 'no' from about four out of five prospects. The trick is to learn how to cope with rejection and focus on the winning outcomes. When we investigate possibilities for promotion or ask for new responsibilities, we may come up against objections or outright refusal. We need to learn from rejections rather than using them as an excuse to stick with the status quo.

Step 6: Make your message clear

Your message is in everything you do and say about your next role. As explained in Chapter 6, your message is a positive, condensed version of your wish list, a one-sentence summary of what you are looking for: the kind of skills you want to use and develop, and the kind of role you will enjoy.

Step 7: Fall forwards

Don't be afraid of making mistakes; it's all part of the process. The important thing is to fall forwards, not backwards; in other words, to learn from your false starts. Keep looking for new angles, new possibilities for your next 'offer'. You will end up very focused, and very clear about what you want to do next. Employers really buy into this level of confidence.

Step 8: Recruit your dream team

Every top sports performer needs a dream team: a coach, a personal trainer, experienced athletes, motivators and managers.

Who can help you? At the very least, recruit some positive-thinking friends to support you through your exploration and your discoveries, and to help you cope with the ups and downs of job search. It's the only way of getting past the constraints we identified in Chapter 3 – the barriers that get in the way, the internal voices that tell you that you won't succeed. The biggest barriers to career change are ones you create yourself.

Step 9: Keep making connections

Successful sales people and recruiters know step 9 well. Set time aside to maintain relationships. Keep careful records of your contacts and keep in touch at least once every 6 months. Cultivate the people who are already at the centre of great networks, the people who know everybody and know what's happening before it happens. The early tip-off often makes the difference between being a leader and being a follower.

The overall message? In the game of survivor, take responsibility for your future. If you want an average career with average career satisfaction, continue the passive route. If you want to create real choices, take control; an employer is responsible for getting the best out of you, but no one will look after your career but you.

Step 10: Step out

Once you've got the key preparation stages sorted out, start thinking about activity. Make sure your plan for the perfect promotion isn't just a textbook event. What training experiences can you arrange? Who do you need to consult or influence? How are you going to begin to increase your exposure? *What are you going to do now that you have finished this book?*

Useful Websites

Unless stated otherwise, these websites provide free and often downloadable information about career development issues.

GENERAL

www.johnleescareers.com
For full details of John Lees's work and a wide range of career development tips

www.rec.uk.com/looking-for-work-portal.htm
John Lees's tips for career changers published on the Recruitment & Employment Confederation's website

www.sr-associates.com
For an online opportunity to take Quintax, the personality measure outlined in Chapter 3.

CAREER MANAGEMENT AND DEVELOPMENT

http://content.monster.co.uk/career_development/
Monster Career Centre with advice and information on career development, salaries and benefits, workplace issues and changing careers

http://education.independent.co.uk/careers_advice/
The *Independent*'s careers advice, mainly aimed at graduates. The site also contains links and information on MBAs

http://jobs.guardian.co.uk/careerscentre/
The *Guardian*'s career centre. Articles on all aspects of career management

www.alljobsuk.com/
Comprehensive Internet signpost in searching for your next career move

www.askmen.co.uk/money/index.html
Lifestyle portal for men. Wide range of articles on career management and issues surrounding the workplace (has an American bias)

www.bbc.co.uk/business/work/index.shtml
Work and careers information

www.careersfair.com/
Job sites, careers advice, recruitment agencies, careers services, courses and professional bodies. Thousands of UK, European and worldwide links

www.careerstorm.com/navigator/
CareerStorm offers online career development tools

www.careers.lon.ac.uk/
Advice, guidance, information, events, links and other services for graduate job seekers

www.careers-portal.co.uk
Online careers service covering advice and information about higher education and alternatives, also choosing and managing your career

www.handbag.com/careers/careerprogression/
Advice for working women covering change your career, improving your salary, enjoy your job, coping with your boss

www.ideasfactory.com/index.htm
Careers insights and advice from real-life professionals and
practical information for careers in the creative field

www.ivillage.co.uk/workcareer
Career advice for women

www.jobpilot.co.uk
European Job Board with career advice and guidance

www.learndirect.co.uk
Advice on courses available online and through UK
universities and colleges

www.lifelonglearning.co.uk/
Information on lifelong learning and the UK government's
initiatives

www.prospects.ac.uk
Graduate careers website. Information on types of jobs and
industries along with careers advice and guidance

www.totaljobs.com/editorial/getadvice/index.shtm
Job board which also contains career management advice
and a salary checker

www.workthing.com/
Jobs and advice split into industry specialisms with
guidance on career development

WORK/LIFE BALANCE

www.dti.gov.uk/work-lifebalance/
UK government website offering advice and guidance on
worklife balance

www.dti.gov.uk/er/workingparents.htm
UK government website offering guidance to working
parents

WORKPLACE ISSUES

www.e-reputation.co.uk/
A collection of free downloads on improving your
communication skills, persuading others and survival tips
in the workplace

**www.hayspersonnel.com/content/candidate/advice/
your_raise.jsp**
Article on negotiating a pay rise. Further articles and links
to careers advice and salary surveys

www.hse.gov.uk/stress/
Health & Safety Executive website on workplace stress

www.officepolitics.co.uk/
Humorous site based on *The Guardian*'s weekend column
authored by Guy Browning about the absurdities of
working life

www.tiger.gov.uk/
Guide to UK employment law

www.workstress.net/
Website covering work-related stress, its causes and how to
eliminate it

Index

10% Principle   89
20/5 Principle   162

achievements   191
appraisals   22, 171–4
auditing your present role
      13

Bach, Richard   180
Ball, Lucille   200
Belbin team types   198
boss, communicating with
      your   161
boss, working with your
      107, 209
boss's thinking style   162–4

cahoot research   215–17
Career Awareness   43,
      205–6
career breaks   216, 218
Career Drivers Exercise   64
career review   40, 41
career traps   164ff.
career, the idea of a   42
Career-Limiting Actions
      165, 184, 208

ceiling, see glass ceiling
change, coping with   54,
      118
changes of career   11
commitment zones   62
communication of self   26,
      105
constraints   47
counter-offers   182, 202
Crane, Thomas   60
critical incidents   26
culture of the organization
      21, 31, 88,
      205

dream team   230
Drucker, Peter   1, 79

early warning system
      89–90
Elevator Pitch, the   177
employer needs checklist
      82

Faust, Bill & Richard   177
Fox, Matthew   135
Frost, Robert   116

glass ceiling   165–6
goal setting   63–4
goals, work and life   134

Herriott, Peter   117
hours of work   16, 42

Ibarra, Herminia   220
individuation   132–3
integrated breakthrough
      219
integrity   220–1
intellectual capital   50

job offers   200
job search   186
Johari Window   105
Jung, Carl   133–3

Kazerounian, Nadine   166
Key Result Areas in a job or
      organization   80–82,
      96, 143, 153, 159, 207
knowledge   50

language   88
leapfrogging   5, 6
learning   61
life balance exercise   140
lifeboat, stocking your
      181–4, 228
Lincoln, Abraham   214
luck   3

managing others   170
manipulative behaviours
      127–8

Manzoni & Barsoux   169
'Me Plc'   228
mentors   29
message, your   50, 230
mobility   30
motivated skills   187
motivation   56, 85, 183

negotiation   175, 201, 212
negotiation, of pay   156
networking   28, 41, 161,
      184–6, 230

OBVIOUS method   7
organization, understanding
      the   25, 37
outcomes, in addition to
      objectives   85–87, 176

Paine, Thomas   142
Pareto principle   95
passivity, in career activity
      10
Pasteur, Louis   55
paternalism   205
Patrick, Lerissa   60
pay   201
pay ranges, estimating   148
pay, and motivation   59,
      143
Pemberton, Carole   117
perfect job, idea of   42
performers, top   12
personal life, impact on   36
personality   51
Piercy, Marge   221
pilot schemes   174

pitch, making your   177
politics, organizational
   28–9, 122–7, 229
Porot, Daniel   18
positioning, conscious or
   unconscious   121, 211
preparation before promotion
   160
prepared responses   181–2
presentations   110–15
promotion possibilities   4
psychological contract   11
Push and pull   181

qualifications   22, 217
quick wins   92, 206
Quintax personality
   instrument   52

redundancy   100, 116–18
rejection   229
retention   174–5
retraining   216–17
rewards   61, 143
Robertson, Stuart   52, 133

San Francisco   45
Sarnoff, David   99

self-awareness   20
self-promotion   100–4
Shackleton   59
Skill Cards   199
skills   1, 16, 50, 187–90
skills triangle   190
SMART objective setting   85
specialising   166–7
sponsors   29
success   55
survey questions   2, 19
survival techniques   118ff.
SWOT analysis   90

team role exercise   192
teams   109
Time stealers   97
Twain, Mark   40

USPs   183

values   53

work/life balance   135
working upwards   27
world of work, changes to
   the   129

Other self-help books from McGraw-Hill

How to Get A Job You'll Love – John Lees
Price: £12.99
ISBN: 0077103823
How To Get A Job You'll Love 2003-04 edition takes a refreshing look at career planning. It teaches you how to think outside the box, tap into your hidden talents and identify what type of career you really want. It seeks to overcome some of the most common mental barriers to changing careers and sets out a five-point plan of action.

Job Interviews: Top Answers to Tough Questions –
Matthew J. Deluca & John Lees
Price: £8.99
ISBN: 0077107047
Job Interviews: top answers to tough questions is your indispensable guide to thriving in any interview situation. 'Top UK Careers Guide John Lees' has joined forces with American careers expert, Matthew J Deluca, to take you through the whole interview process.

Walking Tall: Key steps to total image impact –
Lesley Everett
Price: £9.99
ISBN: 0077099672
Walking Tall is the authoritative guide on how to make and create a positive personal image impact in the workplace. It focuses on recognising the importance of positive non-verbal communication and identifies and sensitively deals with correcting negative 'messages'.

Life Matters: How to Generate Positive Momentum in Every Aspect of your Life – A. Roger Merrill and Rebecca Merrill
Price: £14.99
ISBN: 0071422137
As the home front and the work front become increasingly integrated in contemporary life, success – or failure – in either has an undeniable effect on the other. But it is possible to keep both areas moving forward in positive ways. *Life Matters* show readers how to navigate the critical relationships between time and money, work and family, to create a harmonious, success-enhancing dynamic between each.

Time Management: A Briefcase Book – Marc Mancini
Price: £11.99
ISBN: 0071406107
Time Management provides hands-on techniques and tools for making every minute count as it dispels myths that can actually cost instead of save valuable time. It helps managers match the right time-saving tool to each situation, reveals secrets for anticipating instead of reacting, and explains how any manager can eliminate procrastination.

The Career Survival Guide – Brian O'Connell
Price: £12.99
ISBN: 0071391304
The Career Survival Guide is an indispensable source of expert insight, analysis, and guidance for today's beleaguered and confused corporate citizen. And it offers a gold mine of sure-fire tips on how to find a mentor, how to get and use insider business information, how to read the tea leaves when your job may be on the line, and how to handle corporate politics.

Tools for Success: A Manager's Guide – Suzanne Turner
Price: £9.99
ISBN: 0077107101
Tools for Success is your one-stop guide to all the essential management tools, which will help you to develop the performance of your team and your organisation. A concise, yet comprehensive book, it provides the complete spectrum of management tools from time management, to problem solving, from six sigma to balanced scorecard.

Harvard Business Essentials: Negotiation –
Harvard Business School Press
Price: £14.99
ISBN: 1591391113
Provides practical advice to help any manager broker better deals, and effectively mediate disputes. Discusses a multitude of negotiation topics, including multiparty negotiations, assessing the position of the opposing side, and determining your sources of power and authority in a negotiation. Also, includes useful tips and tools on preparing for negotiation and closing the deal

Harvard Business Essentials: Managing Creativity and
Innovation – Harvard Business School Press
Price: £14.99
ISBN: 1591391121
Managing through change and crisis is difficult in any business environment, let alone ones as turbulent as manager's face today. This timely guide offers authoritative advice on how to recognise the need for organisational change, communicate the vision, prepare for structural change such as M&A, and address emotional responses to downsizing.

**201 Killer Cover Letters – Sandra Podesta
and Andrea Paxton**
Price: £13.99
ISBN: 0071413294
201 Killer Cover Letters provides job seekers with an
unbeatable competitive edge by arming them with sure-fire
sample letters for every job-hunting situation. This CD-ROM
edition of the best-selling guide contains ready-to-download
templates of all 201 letters making it easier than ever for
readers to tailor cover letters to specific situations.

**Becoming A Manager: How New Managers Master the
Challenges of Leadership – Linda A. Hill**
Price: £11.99
ISBN: 1591391822
A business classic, updated with new insights and context
from Hill, one of Harvard's top leadership thinkers and
scholars.
Real voices of real first-year managers that remain fresh and
relevant. These voices of experience give the book not only
authority but a strong sense of humanity.

How To Shine at Work – Linda Dominguez
Price: £11.99
ISBN: 0071408657
A practical, straight-talking guide to thriving in today's
tumultuous workplace.
How to Shine at Work describes 14 sure-fire strategies, as
well as dozens of techniques and tips, for charting a course
through today's work environment and coming out at the
head of the pack.

If you wish to order any of the above books then
please contact our Customer Services Department on
Tel: +44 (0) 1628 502700 Fax: +44 (0) 1628 635895